JUST A STORY FROM AMERICA

A Memoir

ELLIOTT MURPHY

Copyright © 2019 by Elliott Murphy

All rights reserved.

No part of this book may be reproduced in any form or by any electronic or mechanical means, including information storage and retrieval systems, without written permission from the author, except for the use of brief quotations in a book review.

Cover Photo: Jack Mitchell

All interior photos from Elliott Murphy's personal collection © 2019

Contents

Prologue	1
Chapter 1	7
Chapter 2	37
Chapter 3	47
Chapter 4	53
Chapter 5	73
Chapter 6	79
Chapter 7	87
Chapter 8	102
Chapter 9	115
Chapter 10	132
Chapter 11	146
Chapter 12	152
Chapter 13	176
Epilogue	181
Afterword	187
Notes	191
About the Author	199
Also by Elliott Murphy	201

"The world breaks everyone, and afterward, some are strong at the broken places." Ernest Hemingway

"So, we beat on, boats against the current, borne back ceaselessly into the past." F. Scott Fitzgerald

"You've been through all of F. Scott Fitzgerald's books - You're very well read - It's well known." Bob Dylan

Prologue

ELLIOTT MURPHY IS GOING TO BE A MONSTER

"Aquashow" New York City subway poster 1973

"*Elliot Murphy is going to be a monster.*"

That's exactly what the giant New York City subway poster boldly prophesized; no question about it, done deal, in the bag. This sensational all caps quote, printed in fire-engine red, quasi-propaganda style, like something out of the Bolshevik Revolution, was attributed to acclaimed rock writer Lorraine O'Grady of New York's hip journal of record *The Village Voice.* The colossal black and white headshot that nearly filled the entire frame was blown up from another smaller photo inserted into the poster's right-hand margin that pictured me literally *chilling* on the front bumper of a vintage *Rolls Royce*, stylishly dressed in a designer white suit (long before John Travolta would give white suits a whole different spin in *Saturday Night Fever*) and sporting snazzy python skin footwear like my then hero Keith Richards was known to favor. If you *google* Warren Beatty when he played 1930's outlaw Clyde Barrow in the film *Bonnie and Clyde*, you'll see him sitting on a vintage car's bumper holding a *rat-a-tat-tat* machine gun. That *look*, I suppose, was what the photographer was going for as I grasped my sunburst *Fender Stratocaster* guitar firmly in my left hand. Looking back, I noticed that I already had a disquieting sense that this prophecy was not going to play out quite as *monster-like* as all the interested parties were hoping but, for better or worse, this is how I made my entrance onto the world stage, during what was surely a *golden age* of rock music, being part of an East Coast centered music scene that produced legendary artists, timeless records and personally gave me the impetus, the kick-start, for a career that has kept going these forty some-odd years later, albeit in a far different fashion, and on a different continent, from what I must have been imagining when I posed for the photo on that poster ... last century.

Lurking at the bottom of the poster was the *raison d'etre*[1] for the whole deal: the cover to my newly released debut album and, annotated in a sober typeface, *How's The Family is just one of the songs from Elliott Murphy's Aquashow*, followed, of course, by the logo and slogan of my record company: *From Polydor with Pride*. What I did best back then, and still do best, was write and sing introspective rock songs, often from a more literary angle then you might expect judging from what you hear on the radio or *Spotify* but hopefully with just as memorable choruses as the hits of the day; songs that tried to connect the emotional *zeitgeist* of my life with that of our times. Plus, I'm a pretty damn good guitar player when I'm not chilling on the bumper of a *Rolls Royce*. In terms of being part of any linear creative tradition, I tried to stay faithful to my own holy trinity: the Bob Dylan of *Blond on Blond*, the Lou Reed of *Loaded* and the F. Scott Fitzgerald of anything he ever wrote. Terms such as marketing, promotion and publicity were alien to my heroic aspirations, and my sole contribution to this impressive marketing display, this arrogant advertisement, as best I can remember, had been to ask the graphic designer to please modify the front license plate of the Rolls, in a bit of wishful thinking, to read ... *EM*. They agreed.

That poster was the first salvo in an international campaign to promote my album *Aquashow*, wherein my image would be that of a dandy rocker, a modern-day Jay Gatsby with a *Stratocaster* and a musician who dressed and rode in style. Writing and singing of the angst of suburbia in songs such as *How's The Family*, I would chronicle the cultural vapidity of middle class existence, and the disintegration of the American family, none of which, by the way, ever crossed my mind when I sat down to write the ten songs on that album. What I had wanted to do was just write good rock 'n roll songs, songs that made you think *and* boogie; songs that would explain, justify and glorify my own existence on this earth. Just as the Eskimos have no single word for *snow* I didn't know what my subject matter was until the critics defined it for me.

The *back story* of that ad campaign began during an early morning brainstorming session held just weeks before between the promotional team of *Polydor Records* and an expensive Madison Avenue ad agency that sleepy-eyed me reluctantly attended. From what I could fathom, it looked like I was about to be *launched* in a nationwide publicity campaign, as a kind of super-hero come to American to redeem the damned soul of suburbia while having a hit album in the process. I nixed that ad agency's initial proposal of having me actually stroll around New York's crowded *Times Square*, dressed in flowing white robes, with a sign hoisted on my shoulder that asked, *How's The Family?* (the first single from my album) while an accompanying van with mounted loudspeakers would blast out that track's refrain at mega-volume to passing Broadway crowds. But it was clear that the Madison Avenue *madmen* had decided that my public persona was to be that of a literary and sophisticated semi-glam rocker who could easily fit into the format of morning TV talk shows, where I would come forth with pithy and memorable comments on cue. In short, *to boldly go where no ... rockstar ... has gone before.*

It was January 1974 and although the year had opened with the sound of screeching brakes, when President Richard Nixon imposed a fifty-five-mph speed limit on every driver in the nation, in my case the exact opposite was happening. My own life was speeding ahead as vital decisions were being made by my handlers that would impact my future in ways that I could never have envisioned. My album *Aquashow* (at the time only available on black grooved vinyl LPs) was stacked high on record stores shelves across the country, being played on heavy rotation on many FM radio stations, and almost unanimously praised by the rock press and beyond. Once I hooked up with *Steve Leber and David Krebs,* ex-*William Morris* booking agents and now high-powered managers, promo and touring plans materialized began to take shape: I would open concerts for both the legendary British Band the *Kinks* as well as San Francisco's *Jefferson Starship* in theatres and rock venues and start a series of wide ranging interviews ranging from the very serious *Newsweek* to *Sixteen Magazine* who wanted to know my favorite color. Now, nearly half a century later, all that remains from that photo shoot is my 1961 Fender Stratocaster and a faded white suit I really should donate to the *Rock and Roll Hall of Fame*. Obviously, the *Rolls Royce* was never mine to begin with, rented of course, and not really my dream car anyway. They should have used a *Cadillac* or at least a suburban looking station wagon. When I finally got a nice decent advance from my next label RCA Records two years, later I bought a red *MGB* convertible.

What had happened was that my album *Aquashow* had actually already been released with barely any promotion at all just a few months before, and now *Polydor Records*, my well-meaning but, at the time, hapless record company, was furiously trying to out-run the *tsunami* of media attention the album was generating all on its own. They were taken completely by surprise when suddenly my name seemed to be everywhere, most notably in an iconic review in *Rolling Stone* right next to Bruce Springsteen's second album *The Wild, The Innocent, and E-Street shuffle* that seemed to proclaim we were both in the running as "the new Bob Dylan. On the west coast, Robert Hilburn was lauding *Aquashow* in the *LA Times*, and more rave reviews were coming in on almost a daily basis from all over. Luckily for me, the head of *Polydor* public relations, a sensitive and insightful soul name Lloyd Gellasen, had seen the promise in *Aquashow* long before anyone else at the label and, in an understated campaign, had tirelessly kept reaching out to important journalists. When the good reviews started coming in Lloyd was a hero ... until Polydor fired him a few years later. To this day, I am indebted to Lloyd for all his efforts on my behalf. They say when a recording artist starts to build a fan base he had better begin with his record company and Lloyd was my first fan. For months after the album's release, a few times a week Lloyd would escort me to lunch with yet another journalist and I soon discovered that a few *Johnny Walker Black* Scotch on the rocks helped those interviews flow effortlessly.

So, Polydor was in a panic to get its promo troops on the move and actually start selling some albums and a hometown attack on New York's pubic transport system was launched. Within weeks of that ad agency conference, the posters were pasted up two by two in subway stations all over Manhattan. I first came face to face with my Gatsby*esque* self at the Bleecker Street stop, the epicenter of *Green-*

wich Village, where Jimi Hendrix had played at the *Café a Go Go* back in the 1960's. As I stood there in front of *me*, I become conscious that someone was standing next to me, a hippie caught in a time-warp, a survivor of the summer of love, who was as glued to that poster as I was. In truth, the guy was probably only in his forties, but he seemed ancient to me with his graying long hair and faded tie-dyed clothes. I seem to remember him wearing a *Grateful Dead* T-shirt but that could be just my enhanced memory. Anyway, we stood next to each other, until that moment came when he turned and noticed me and with a visible jolt of recognition, pointed to me and then to the guy in the poster. I nodded my head and was somewhat taken aback when a sincere and sorrowful expression came over the guy's face. "Good luck man," he said solemnly without the slightest trace of enthusiasm before moving on his way. I remember standing there transfixed until the subway station emptied out and I was alone. Anxiety tingled down my spine. I was twenty-four years old.

Chapter One

HOW'S THE FAMILY

| Cover of original "Aquashow" program 1953

We're so East Coast – So here's a toast – Here's to everything that I wanted the most ... (Change Will Come)

I come from an East Coast show business family. Throughout the nineteen-fifties, my father, Elliott Murphy Sr., produced a wildly successful outdoor *spectacle* on the site of New York's 1939 World's Fair in a sprawling amphitheater called *The Aquashow*. Six-thousand seats arched around an Olympic sized swimming pool where a bevy of *Aquadorables* executed synchronized ballet swimming, where now-forgotten comics such as Jack Carter and Henny Youngman told corny jokes and, most importantly, where still legendary orchestra leaders, iconic names such as Duke Ellington and Cab Callaway, jazzed it all up big band style, as fireworks lit up the Flushing, Queens sky. Even Francis Ford Coppola's father, Carmine Coppola, who went on to contribute to the soundtrack of both *The Godfather* and *Apocalypse Now* is credited in one of the programs resting in my dusty archives. *Elliott Murphy's Aquashow,* ran for six nights a week in the summer season for over ten years and made my father rich and famous for a while and its memory lived on as the *glory days* of the Murphy family whenever we gathered together for holidays. As you might imagine, *The Aquashow* was a magical place to be around as a child, especially when you're the son of the boss. There were dancing monkeys on floating logs, dozens of silver painted canoes traversing the pool, beautiful swimmers in sparkly swimsuits, clown divers, high divers, spotlights galore, all bathed in show business glamor. Still, my father taught me a lesson that I have carried with me to this day, that in this *business* luck runs much of the *show*. If it rained, nobody came.

My dad came from Brooklyn where his own father, an Irish immigrant and former English Army soldier in colonial India and the Boer War, worked as a blacksmith and later garage owner who lost most everything he had worked so hard for in the great depression of the 1930's when he couldn't pay the newly raised taxes on his property. Things got so desperate that he would send his children searching for pieces of coal, fallen from passing train engines, scattered down by railroad tracks, to stoke the family heater and keep them all warm on winter nights. This poignant image stuck with me and I used it in a line from my song *On Elvis Presley's Birthday*, which my father, long gone from this earth, never heard. My grandfather, James William Murphy, was an Irish Catholic and his wife Lillian, an immigrant from Northern Ireland, was Protestant, and apparently, they could never make peace on what religion to raise their kids in, which was good for me because by the time I came around, in my family at least, going to church was much less vital to our spiritual growth than, say, going to a fine restaurant or catching the latest Hollywood movie. My father was a self-made man and, not surprisingly, a lifelong *Republican*, albeit of that now-extinct liberal northeast variety, who although they might not like labor unions telling them how to run their business or paying rising income taxes or believing in the social benefits of welfare, were generally socially moderate and detested the racist southern *Democrats* – called *Dixiecrats* back then – who ruled the Senate and fought integration at every turn. I know my dad adored President Eisenhower as we had *I LIKE IKE* buttons scattered around the house long after the famed General's last presidential campaign was over and I don't know if he voted for ultra-conservative Republican Barry Goldwater in the 1965 presidential election, but I do remember that the first time I saw my father's tears was when my family solemnly watched the seemingly endless funeral cortege of John F. Kennedy on our black and white *Zenith* TV.

Today, his species of *Rockefeller*[1] *Republicans* seems to have become extinct, disappearing along with much of the flaunted *American Dream* of his time, a credo to which he wholly subscribed. My dad was a patriot and fierce eagle emblems adorned our house in a pre-Vietnam world where we believed our leaders always, always, always told the truth. As far as I'm concerned, the *Father Knows Best*[2] era of my country began with George Washington and ended sometime around LBJ and Nixon; each from a different political party, both secretly escalating the Vietnam War. In public, my father had a somewhat stiff military bearing, which I suppose he inherited from his own father, a twenty-year veteran of the British army. A man of habit, he consistently wore conservative Brooks Brothers suits and striped rep ties, rarely cursed except when his canker sores were acting up (an affliction I seem to have inherited), and faithfully ate shrimp cocktails, well-done *minute steaks* topped with *A1 sauce*, and vanilla *Louis Sherry* ice cream, a diet that may have been his undoing. The most useful piece of advice my father gave me, and keep in mind that he was a staunch Republican patriot, was to stay out of the army if I could (he did so by working in the Brooklyn Navy Yard during WWII). He said his own father, an English army veteran who survived the horrendous *Siege of Ladysmith* during the Boer War, passed that advice on to him and now I tell the same thing to my own son Gaspard, who grew up in France, went to college in America and doesn't know anybody who ever joined either country's army. I wanted to name my son *Elliott Murphy III,* but my French wife Françoise insisted *non!* Names followed by numerals are shunned in France because Aristocrats, even from Brooklyn origins I suppose, still risk losing their heads come the next revolution.

When my father found fame and fortune with the success of his *Aquashow* back in the 1950's, he moved his family from Jackson Heights, Queens, to Garden City, a conservative Long Island upper-middle class village in affluent Nassau County. The town itself was originally conceived by 19th century department store magnate A.T. Stewart as a proper place for his employees to live in the dozen or so Victorian houses he built, now reverently referred to as *disciple* houses by the natives. Stewart, being a very religious Scot Protestant immigrant, also built the dark and towering Episcopalian cathedral where he and his employee could worship and where I was baptized in 1949 shortly after my birth. On that occasion, my father's publicist, who was Jewish, came with a medallion that he had gotten in Rome, blessed by the pope himself and said it would bring me luck. I was baptized Episcopalian with a blessing by the Catholic pope delivered by a Jewish press agent so how could I have anything *but* good luck? Conservative Garden City was also noted for its fine public schools, which I attended reluctantly and without distinction, but my parents were not academics, neither one possessing a college degree, and so high marks on report cards didn't account for much around my house. I barely scraped by before finally graduating from Garden City High School in 1967. The school does boast a few notable alumni: *All My Children* TV star Sue Lucci from my sister's class, TV host and singer John Tesch from my brother's, former US Secretary of Energy Steven Chu from a grade above me, and, I suppose, me from my own.

    My family could never really decide what religion we wanted to adhere to but one thing was sure, it was not going to be Catholic. The local parish priest in Brooklyn had refused to allow my paternal grandfather to be buried in the church cemetery there on account of him committing the unpardonable sin of not faithfully bringing his kids to mass every week. And my mother had a visceral anti-Catholic bias which apparently had something to do with birth control. She also thought that many of the priests were pedophiles and she wasn't so wrong there. But I had no problems with the Catholics in my town because the wildest Garden City girls, mostly Irish and Italian, seemed to be just that, and years later, my first fledgling band shows would be at *St, Josephs* church where the nuns would separate couples who danced too close together. I do remember those rare Sundays when we would attend church at the village's gothic Episcopalian cathedral and then retreat to the *Garden City Hotel* for a formal breakfast, where fresh squeezed Orange Juice was served in small glasses resting on crushed ice and we feasted on waffles with real maple syrup or perfectly poached eggs. I don't remember a word of the Episcopal sermons, but I do remember those gala breakfasts, sitting at a large round table, my father in a *Brooks Brothers* suit and a white handkerchief peeking from his breast pocket, the celebrity of the town in my eyes, and my beautiful and glamorous mother, smartly dressed from *Saks Fifth Avenue,* her flaming red hair perfectly coiffed, keeping careful watch on her children's table manners. I cherished meals with my family, when we were all together, because my father loved to tell stories as we ate, mostly those from growing up in Brooklyn, most probably enhanced in the telling; especially those about my grandfather who I never met, when a gargantuan work horse sat on him while he was shoeing it and he had to hit it repeatedly with a hammer on the butt and of him rescuing swimmers caught in rip tides on *Coney Island*. These stories enraptured me, forever part of my imagination's permanent collection, and now, one could say, that's what I do for a living, telling my own stories, standing on stage with a guitar strapped across my shoulder. Regrettably, I was too young, to ask my father those questions every son would like to ask when he's no longer around, what you should do after failing when you can't gather the strength to start over again. But I do remember him always saying to me, *Jimmy*[3], *the whole world's talking about you!* And that mantra has gotten me through many a dark day.

When I was twelve he bought me a biography of Clarence Darrow, the legendary 1920's attorney perhaps best known as the defense lawyer in the *Scopes Monkey* trial, wherein a Tennessee high school teacher was arrested for teaching Darwin's theory of evolution in a public school. From what I watch on *CNN* these days, Southern Baptist mentality has not changed that much. My father didn't want me to have to live by my wits, like he had, constantly reinventing himself, but rather to get a solid education and a secure career like partner in a law firm. I still admire Clarence Darrow, and always found his use of the insanity plea in the *Leopold and Loeb thrill killers* case even more interesting, and many years later, during my *dark days* of the 1980's, I even did work for nearly two years at a prestigious Manhattan law firm as a legal assistant and learned everything I needed to know about contracts, a fickle judge's whims and why I didn't want to become a lawyer.

With his first flush of money, after his *Aquashow* became successful following a disastrous initial season, my father bought himself a customized Cadillac with a see-through bubble roof that was profiled in *New Yorker* magazine. He made an appearance on the

Ed Sullivan Show[4] and had his own table at *Sardi's* restaurant, a Broadway show biz mecca of his day and ours, his name proudly displayed on a brass plaque right above his usual table. I think my father enjoyed his new-found celebrity but not being reminded of his humble origins on Fort Hamilton Parkway, Brooklyn, where he grew up over his family's garage. I remember as a child being with him in Mineola, one of Garden City's less affluent neighboring towns, buying the *Sunday New York Times* when an old classmate from Erasmus High School recognized him. I had the distinct impression, even at that young age, that my father was trying to avoid him, and we left the store quickly. Ironically, the beginnings of my own music career, twenty years later in the early seventies, was all about embracing my American style *bourgeoise* origins with songs like *White Middle Class Blues* and *How's the Family*.

After my father's *Aquashow* was bushwhacked by the lengthy construction of the Long Island Expressway[5], and it's seemingly *express* lack of exits to the amphitheater's huge parking lot, my father gave all that up, stacked a dozen or so canoes and a hundred boxes of sparkly swimsuits in our garage, and bought a floor-through restaurant in Garden City, the upper middle-class village where we lived in grand style for a while. His restaurant was located on the top floor of the *Franklin National Bank* building in Roosevelt Field[6] and he called it *Elliott Murphy's Sky Club* because he liked to see his name attached to the things he owned and often wore the same gold monogramed cufflinks that I also wore on the cover of my second album *Lost Generation*. The *Sky Club* overlooked Roosevelt Field, located at Garden City's eastern border, almost the exact spot from where Charles Lindbergh took off from on his historic 1927 flight to France in the windowless *Spirit of St. Louis*. Roosevelt Field had since evolved from a pioneering airfield to a pioneering shopping center. The march of progress! I took the same direction as Lindbergh[7], albeit in a much bigger plane and a few more windows, some sixty years later.

My father' restaurant, *The Sky Club*, was the epicenter of Nassau

County's intense political activity and New York governor Nelson Rockefeller, Senator Robert F. Kennedy and other dignitaries of the time often came to speak at exclusive men's only *Sky Island Club* lunches. I have a somewhat shocking photo of a striptease artist performing at one of these lunches right in front of Bobby Kennedy and my Dad; both of them looking quite content to be there! My father's personal lawyer and confidant was ex-congressman Leonard Hall, once the chairman of the Republican National Committee and who told my father in confidence that the 1960 presidential campaign had been stolen from them by Joe Kennedy. Who knows? Len Hall was also the law partner of William Casey, who would later become Director of the CIA under Ronald Reagan. According to Bob Woodward, Bill Casey, held the secrets to the *Iran-Contra* affair but conveniently died before he could be called to testify before Congress. But as a teenager, any political wheeling and dealing going on at my father's restaurant was not nearly as fascinating to me as were the musical elements of the place. There were always instruments set up on its small circular bandstand, and the weekend *headliner* was a blind organist named Hank Faller who played a *mean* Hammond B3 organ, ironically, the *go-to* keyboard of rock 'n roll[8]. My parents would dance when Hank played their favorite song *I Wish You Love*[9] and my brother, my sister and I would sit at one of the ringside tables surrounding the dance floor, sipping our *Shirley Temple* faux-cocktails, and probably embarrassed by their display of affection and graceful moves. Now, when we think back to those lost tender moments between our parents, we get teary-eyed.

Hank Faller showed me how that massive double keyboard instrument worked and even talked my father into buying his own Hammond B3 Organ for our three-story house in Garden City, set back on four acres of land with a brick wall and iron gates straddling the entrance. Not quite a mansion like today's *one-percenters* call home but still pretty damn affluent for its time. Talking my father into buying that Hammond organ was probably not so difficult because he had a love of musical instruments and spread throughout that vast house was quite a collection: a baby grand piano, a pump action church organ, a genuine *player* piano with *rolls* of music, a xylophone, an accordion, a trumpet, and, later of course, numerous guitars. Even before I was old enough to fool around with these *real* instruments, every Christmas I would usually find a few plastic *Eminee* toy musical instruments, waiting for me under the tree. They weren't real of course, but I loved them just the same and made lots of noise, some of it even musical, as I strolled around the house. Although it may have been evident to my parents that I was undoubtedly a musical prodigy, my talents were clearly passed over when I attended Stewart School[10] grammar school, where we had a weekly music class, presided over by a dominating *battle-axe* of a music teacher who looked like the society matron straight out of a Marx Brothers film. At the beginning of each school year we were separated into *listeners* and *singers* based upon our performance in a stressful audition wherein that teacher would play scales on the piano while each student would try their best to sing the matching harmonic intervals, *Hel-lo, Hel-lo,* and be judged accordingly. It was a terrifying experience, my first case of stage fright and believe it or not, I was made a ... *listener!* But I guarantee you, out of all the thousands of Garden City grammar school kids who passed through that music teacher's class, I well may the only one who has gone on to make a living as a *bonified* singer.

At around eleven years old, I took trumpet lessons but couldn't quite get the feel of the instrument and, Louis Armstrong notwithstanding, didn't think it was too cool. Actually, I more liked the idea of pounding on a shiny pearl and chrome set of drums, vis-à-vis Gene Krupa, but fortunately my parents talked me out of that. To this day, I have great sympathy for the parents of young drummers, who must put up with the constant *rat-a-tat-tat* of their kids beating out *paradiddles*. School and I did not get along, and as I was having trouble paying attention and often acting up in class this led to regular appointments with the school psychologist where I would be asked to stare at ink blots[11] and then describe what I imagined I saw.

Mostly I saw pairs of women breasts, but I didn't dare say it. Today, they call what I had *attention deficit disorder* and prescribe calming medications like *Ritalin* while researchers search for its genetic cause. But I could have told them that the true cause lies not in the *DNA* of the kids but in the *DNA* of the school system itself, which is boring enough to drive any kid, not willing to become a robot, crazy! I must confess that I hated nearly every day of school, except for those rare times when I had to write a short story in English class or the one year of music theory I took as a senior and when I just barely managed to graduate from High School in 1967 it really felt like I was finally let out of prison after years of planning my escape.

Anyway, when I was twelve my intuitive mom Josephine, a natural-born *iconoclast*, thought that since I liked Elvis Presley so much when I saw him on *The Ed Sullivan Show* on TV, perhaps I would do better with the guitar then playing trumpet in the school band and she decided we would take lessons together at *Quigley's Music Center* in New Hyde Park. And *Voila!* Me and all things *guitar* was love at first sight; just the smell of a guitar case turned me on, and I found the wide variety of guitar picks and straps spellbinding and I took to the instrument like I had taken to ice cream or literature or, some years later, to sex. Playing the guitar, to me at least, was a combination of all three. Mrs. Quigley, our teacher, was young, attractive and patient and taught my mother and I from the standard lexicon of folk songs such as *Coming 'Round the Mountain* and *My Darling Clementine*. I won't bore you with the history of my *pilgrim's progress,* but I went on to study jazz guitar at the Garden City Music Center with a cool teacher who always seemed hung over from his cocktail lounge gigs the night before and even classical guitar lessons later on with another teacher who was more concerned with my fingernail care then my approach to *Bach*. In truth, like almost all rock 'n roll musicians of my generation, most of what I learned I had to teach myself, playing 45 rpm singles over and over until I could figure out the chords and the words. Today, any song my son Gaspard wants to learn, he merely has to *Google* its name and there it is, verse, chorus and guitar chords, all the mystery shot to hell while I must have worn out my seven inch 45rpm of *Louie Louie* trying to find the hidden dirty words; although still, to this day, I'm not sure if there really were any there.

There was a folk boom going on in the early sixties and I was a fan of *The Kingston Trio, Peter, Paul and Mary* and other successful folk groups of the day. Two things, both equally important, changed my life's direction around that time. That Christmas, my sister Michelle, gave me Bob Dylan's first album as a present. She had been to see him perform in concert at Princeton University and although, according to her, the public had not been very enthusiastic and mocked his then scruffy appearance, she was completely enthralled. My favorite song on Dylan's first album was *House of the Rising Sun* and when the *Animals* version came out a few years later I already knew how to sing and play it by heart. And I still occasionally play it at my own shows over fifty years later. *There is a house in New Orleans* ... And the other thing was that I bought my first guitar strap, which allowed me to play the instrument standing up and even singing into a microphone. You can't imagine what a game changer that was.

Like almost every U.S. rock musician biography you're ever going to read, I was putting together bands all through junior and senior high school but most times, I was rarely the singer, perhaps still discouraged by my grammar school music teacher's vilification. My *epiphany* came when I sixteen, down in my band mate Tommy Tucker's basement one afternoon after school, showing off my guitar skills for two fine looking girls of our own age who kept begging me to sing something for them, promising kisses if I did. And so, I stood up, put the guitar strap over my shoulder, strummed a C–Am–F–G chord progression and took a shot at the intro of Dion's *Runaround Sue,* "Here's my story it's sad but true ..." and those girls swooned and screeched, and each gave me a long kiss on the mouth and goddamn if I didn't see my future career path unfold before me, lined with kisses from more beautiful girls. And I can tell you now, as Frank Sinatra once sang *not in a shy way*, I've certainly had my share. All thanks to Dion.

Garden City was safe, predictable and boring; the nearest movie theaters were in bordering Hempstead, which, with its large black population made many of the all-white GC residents nervous. For adolescent thrills my buddies and I hung out in the sinister looking, at least to our white-middle class eyes, Hempstead Bus Terminal, a grimy place full of diesel fumes and illicit charms, where closet sized kiosks sold ivory handled switch blades, hot dogs and R&B records and where I bought the 45rpm single of *Shout* by *The Isley Brothers* that I still play to this day. At our most adventurous, we tried sneaking our way into the neighboring *Fine Arts* movie theater via the fire exit, in anticipation of glimpsing a bit of forbidden female flesh in avant-garde European films such as *I Am Curious Yellow*[12]. But once I crossed Garden City's borders, my favorite hang-out, hands down, was the now closed Hempstead branch of *Sam Ash Music*, a musical instrument store where, depending on the mood of the salesman, I could try out *Fender*, *Gibson* and *Gretsch* guitars and show my prowess with a few licks of the Ventures' 1960 hit instrumental *Walk Don't Run*. I bought many a guitar and amp there that I wish I had today and wonder in whose hands they are now.

In spite of the convenient commute from Garden City to Manhattan via the Long Island Rail Road, my father rarely took the train, always preferring to drive his 1962 maroon *Cadillac Fleetwood* anywhere he needed to go. And being a Brooklyn *homeboy*, he rarely strayed beyond Long Island and the five boroughs of New York City. Trained as a mechanic and engineer, he had a well-stocked *Sears & Roebuck* toolbox and when he was anxious about money, or so recollects my mother, he would go down to his basement workshop, take apart his children's bicycles, fix whatever was wrong, shine them up, and put them back in the garage. Once, when I must have been about eight, he single-handedly built a soapbox[13] racer from wooden fruit crates and discarded baby carriage wheels, mounted it all on a chassis made of two by fours, and painted it white with *Murphy Special* logos in bright red script on the sides. It was stunning! We pushed it around the parking lot of a nearby country club, one of three in the village, hardly the *Dead-End Kids*[14] but still as close to my father's Brooklyn roots as our upper middle-class milieu allowed. When my father would rake and burn piles of fallen autumn leaves (a practice long forbidden I hear now) on our spacious side yards, he would take large baking potatoes with a *ten-penny* nail pushed through and bury them deep in the midst of the smoldering leaves. We'd eat them whole, sprinkling salt and biting down hard through the charred potato skins. My dad called each cooked potato a *mickey* and said his own father had taught him how. And that's about all of my Irish roots that has been passed down to me. Alas, in Paris, there were no piles of burning leaves, and thus no *mickey* heritage to pass on to my own son Gaspard. The only Mickey he knows is a mouse from nearby *Euro Disney*.

    My Garden City bands came and went and with each one my repertoire increased, as my chops improved. There were *The Daytonas* with future *Lifetime* TV CEO Doug McCormick on bass guitar, where I played surf music, and *The Rapscallions* with talented lead singer Jan Rundlett, which won the 1966 *New York State Battle of the Bands* with our finger snapping version of the Shangri-La's *Walking in the Sand*. Then came the second British invasion in the late 1960's, and I quickly assumed the role of a Long Island guitar hero, who thought Eric Clapton *was* God[15], Jeff Beck and Jimmy Page true wizards, and, of course, Jimi Hendrix, in another class entirely. Clapton, Beck and Page I could copy with passable results, but Hendrix was in another league, the first true rock god who soared through the rock 'n roll skies before crashing down to earth and choking to death on his own vomit, at the pitifully young age of 27, a portent of many sad endings yet to come in the kingdom of rock. During the late sixties, I formed heavy rock bands with names like *Stud* and *Bullfrog* and even the biblical themed *King James Version*, playing all the beer joints on Hempstead Turnpike with sawdust on the floor that catered to the local *Hofstra College* crowd. As my bands moved up the food chain we started playing regular gigs at the mafia owned clubs in Long Beach where you were afraid to ask to get paid. Whenever I could afford it, I went to see concerts at Bill Graham's *Fillmore East*, getting plenty stoned on the thirty-minute drive into the city on the Long Island Expressway beforehand. I remember seeing *Derek and The Dominos,* Eric Clapton's post-*Cream* band at the *Capitol Theater* in nearby Westchester County and thinking his drummer, Jim Gordon, had the most contagious *swing* of any drummer I had ever heard. To my astonishment, five years later Jim Gordon himself would be playing drums on my second album, *Lost Generation,* recorded at LA's famed Elektra Studios where the Doors recorded *Light My Fire,* and a few years after that he was in prison for life, having killed his mother with a hammer during a psychotic episode. And then in 1977, I would be playing at that same *Capitol Theater* myself, promoting my fourth album *Just a story from America*. Without a doubt, I *saw my future before it saw me*.

My father's *Sky Club* was a vast restaurant with wall-to-wall windows overlooking Old Country Road, with large private rooms for Weddings, Bar Mitzvahs and College *mixers*[16] and a famous French chef who went on to run the kitchen at the *Windows of the World* restaurant atop one of the *World Trade Center,* later destroyed in the 9/11 terrorist attack. Although my father dutifully attended the *Sky Island Club* luncheons with political luminaries of the day, I had the feeling that he much preferred to hang out with his Puerto Rican busboys in the restaurant parking lot. Once I witnessed him do just that close up when one of those dishwashers bought a *Honda* motorcycle and allowed my father to whip around the parking lot on it with his terrified son, me, hanging on in back. My father's spiritual mentor was minister Norman Vincent Peale author of the best-selling motivational book, *The Power of Positive Thinking.* I never once saw my father drunk nor do I remember him ever smoking and at home he might have a few beers with dinner but that was it. I should have followed his example ...

Around the time I entered third grade, my family moved,

upgrading to one of the finest Garden City residences, a three-story antebellum style mansion with four gargantuan columns standing like sentinels at the entrance, a screened-in porch the size of a living room and a back staircase for maids. I was amazed to see how much this stately wood shingled house bore an uncanny resemblance to Elvis Presley's own *Graceland* mansion outside Memphis, Tennessee, when I made a pilgrimage there many years later. There were other formidable structures on our nearly four acres of land as well; a double garage, gardening and tool sheds, and a romantic white gazebo. The vegetable and fruit gardens were tended by an Italian gardener with a thick accent and powerful arms, Sam Gennaro, who made his own wine in our cellar and once stepped in a hornet's nest. All of this, my childhood *universe,* was protected by an ochre brick wall, taller than I was, and the only house in Garden City to have such a *fortification.* Two rotting horse pulled sleigh carriages sat behind the garage, which my father had bought in the hopes of hitching horses during the next snowstorm, too late finding out that such a thing was forbidden by a village ordinance. He loved horses and sent his children to *The Thomas School of Horsemanship* each summer where we learned to jump and compete in horse shows, and where on *parent's day* he would spend hours inside the stables, no doubt a reminder of his father's blacksmith shop back in Brooklyn. As F. Scott Fitzgerald noted, we are "... *borne back ceaselessly into the past"* and to this day, I love the smell of horses and when I lived in Manhattan, on dark days I would walk up to Central Park South just to hang out among the horse drawn carriages which trotted tourists through the park and breathe in their musky odor.

The 10th Street house (that's what we still call it) was built in the roaring 1920's and in the basement's wine cellar, risqué graffiti and drawings from Prohibition days were scrawled on the wooden wine racks that lined the walls. Perhaps F. Scott Fitzgerald had come there to drink illicitly when he lived in nearby Great Neck and or at least that's what I fantasized when I fell in love with great American novels at an early age. At twelve I had already read Steinbeck's *East of Eden* (after seeing the James Dean film on TV) and soon after came *The Great Gatsby*, Hemingway's *The Old Man and the Sea*, Saroyan's *The Human Comedy* and Mark Twain's *Huckleberry Finn*. I have never stopped reading although now it seems I spend more time looking at movies on my computer than at real books in my hand. My son Gaspard, who did very well in the challenging French academic system with its gladiatorial BAC exam at the end of Lycée (high school), tells me he has hardly any interest in reading novels and my mother says she had to stop reading because she has no memory left and always has to start over from the beginning each time she picks ups a book. She thinks that a *Kindle* is something a fireplace does with logs.

In our big house, I watched totally entranced as The Beatles performed on the Ed Sullivan television show – an often noted epiphany for nearly every rock musician of my generation[17] – and, after buying *Beatle Boots* at Flagg Brothers shoe store, I started rehearsing the easier *Beatles* tunes such as *Twist and Shout* with my bands down in our *finished* basement (where I also brought my girlfriends to make-out). And also, in this grand house in the autumn of 1965, sometime between the deaths of John and Robert Kennedy, my own father died, leaving us nearly broke and forced to move to a much smaller home but still, fortunately I suppose, within the boundaries of Garden City. In the fractured years after we moved, when there was no center to my family or my country, torn apart by the Vietnam War, I often went back to the grand old place at night, stealthily climbing over that wall that ultimately could not protect us from tragedy, and sat on the ground in the dark for hours, staring up at the windows of what once was my parents' bedroom, unable to comprehend why my world had been blown apart and still unable to accept that it would never be what it once was, ever again.

When I was about ten, I had a dream that my father had died, and I ran upstairs to the third floor in tears, desperate to find him and my mother. It must have been close to midnight, I suppose, and they were up on the top third floor, probably figuring out how to organize one of the many rooms in their home. I distinctly remember my father taking me into his arms, drying my tears and assuring me that he was not going to die. I can even remember his comforting smile. Then, six years later he did die suddenly and brutally of a heart attack in that same house in his own bedroom on the second floor. My mother came to get me in the middle of it. There's more that happened that night, sights and sounds that haunt me to this day, that I will get to because I can only revisit that nightmare in short episodes or I'll start to panic, even now, fifty years later. Shrinks call it *post-traumatic stress syndrome*. I call it a permanent heartbreak.

The morning after my father died, my mother woke my younger brother Matthew to tell him the dreadful news. I can only imagine what that must have been like, surely almost unbearable for her and now, as a parent myself, I am in awe of the courage it took, just hours after her husband died. I can still hear my brother's sobbing - that's what woke me up the next morning after finally having fallen asleep on a couch in the living room, and finding the house full of friends, family and funeral workers. Away studying at *Alfred University*, my sister Michelle fainted in her dorm when told the news of her father's death and my mother's father, Papa Wilson, drove upstate to bring her home; it must have been a horrible eight hours in the car for her, waiting to come home to a void.

In 1968, I was driving the *Garden City Florist* delivery van. It was three years after my father's death and we had moved houses, now living on Bayberry Avenue in a modest section of Garden City, if you can even say such a place exists in what for all intents and purposes was, and still is, a very affluent town. I'm sure there must have been families with money problems, but nothing was evident when you'd drive through those tree lined streets, with fine looking homes and manicured lawns, two or even three cars in the driveway. By now, I was going to *Nassau Community College* at night to avoid being drafted into the army, handed an M16 rifle and sent packing to Vietnam and driving the delivery van during the day to make some money. Thing were bad at home. Slim, my mother's second husband,

and I did not get along. He grew up poor, worked construction all his life, and thought I was some kind of a spoiled hippy, who didn't show enough respect for his country. And considering the debacle of the Vietnam War, where it has been proven that the US government was consistently lying to its citizens[18], he was right on that. One evening Slim walked into the house as I was watching the Kent State shootings[19] being reported on the evening news. "They should have used machine guns," were his words verbatim, before walking into the bedroom and slamming the door shut. Another time, when he dropped by after his usual three Martini lunch, I was talking on the wall phone in the kitchen. Glaring at me and saying nothing, he pulled a pair of scissors out of the drawer, worn-in red kitchen shears that had been in our family as long as I could remember, and cut the coiled phone line before silently walking away leaving me standing there with the dead phone in my hands. I was frozen with fury. Years later, my mother made Slim apologize to me for how badly he had treated me, and he did, in a way, while the three of us stood awkwardly on a corner in front of her apartment on York Ave. in Manhattan. But more than a vindication, it was just embarrassing, and it was the last time I ever saw Slim. I shrugged my shoulders and said *don't worry about it* but harbored the resentment for years. Probably still do.

Debbie Haas, a very cute girl my age, lived down the street from us when we lived in the big house. Her father was a successful doctor with a large practice. I kissed her once on her front lawn when I was 13 or something, real first kiss I ever had and I had a crush on her all through high school. Then her own father died a year after my own, another fatal heart attack come out of nowhere. The florist where I worked received numerous orders funeral wreaths and flower arrangements and when they were to be delivered to the funeral home where Debbie's father lay, I would take the rear entrance, and drop them off quickly, hoping I wouldn't see her or any of my classmates. I wasn't ready to face another funeral.

As fate would have it, I've been to quite a few funerals in Paris.

The most moving one, the one that touched me the deepest, was for the actress Elizabeth Catroux, one of my wife Françoise' best friends, and, like her, a graduate of the *Conservatoire national d'art dramatique de Paris*, the most prestigious acting school in Paris. Elizabeth had died suddenly, just in her fifties, leaving a husband and two sons behind. This *tres triste* funeral was held in *Pere La Chaise*, which is where Jim Morrison is buried, Chopin too, and maybe me some day. There is an enormous crematorium there, built over a century ago, and that's where the packed service was held. After a protestant minister spoke (Elizabeth was one of those rare non-Catholic French) many of her friends contributed their own eulogies as well. Elizabeth had not outlived her own mother, a well-known French theater actress herself, who sat close to her daughter's coffin and that was really crushing to see. When the speeches were through and there was nothing left to say but *au revoir,* Elizabeth's coffin was lifted onto a kind of inclined conveyer belt, which brought it to an opening in the wall behind the podium where it would be lowered into the waiting flames and cremated. As the coffin was slowly moving along, we all began to slowly walk out, there must have been a few hundred of us, and then someone, a fellow actress who just couldn't contain her grief any longer, loudly shouted her name *Elizabeth! Elizabeth!* Immediately others followed in suit, her name echoing over and over on the stone walls of that crematorium, like a Greek chorus, and then all of us began to applaud loudly, cheering until the coffin disappeared. My wife and I were both openly weeping as tears dripped to the crematorium's marble floor. Fire and *rain* filled that dark hall as Elizabeth left the stage for the last time and received the standing ovation every performer lives for.

My parents believed life was for the living and so my father's funeral, held at a local Garden City funeral parlor, was a somber affair with a closed casket and no eulogy that I can remember. Many of the local political dignitaries that he counted among his friends came by to pay their respects silently while signing their name in the guest book. Personally, I think Elliott Murphy Sr. deserved more *pomp and circumstance* then that regardless of what my mother believed; the man should have gone out in style because that was what he was about. After all, he was in show business! Well, at least I think I would have liked that better, because maybe it would have put some closure on his death for me. But I was just sixteen and my mother was running the show now. We buried my father in *Greenwood Cemetery* in Brooklyn, not far from where he grew up, and there was not even a marker placed over his grave. I remember the trip there and back, worst limousine ride of my life.

Within a year of saying goodbye forever to my beloved father, I said hello to Slim, who was to become my brutish step-father. I only had my music to keep me afloat as my family sank into a sea of continual crisis as my mother struggled with the bankruptcy of the restaurant and chronic depression of her own. After finally closing the large glass double doors of *The Sky Club* for good, after a dismal New Year's Eve, she began to work as a salesperson in a discount jewelry store on the first floor of that same building. I don't know how she survived it. We went from a *Cadillac Fleetwood* with air conditioning (which was rare in those days) to a crappy *Ford Maverick* with roll up windows, my nomination for the worst American car ever manufactured. My family's story is a sad one but of course, plenty of families have had it so much worse than us and life does go on and we have no choice but to learn to live with the pain of losing someone we love, someone we couldn't imagine living without. How do we survive such losses? I'm still not sure but I know that in my case at least, my saving grace was that I just kept putting bands together; almost like putting a family back together.

In 1966, a year later, the only festive moment I can remember for my own family was when my band *The Rapscallions* won the *New York State Battle of the Bands* at Eisenhower Park in Nassau County and later at another park in Westchester County. We were promised a recording contract and to be part of the historic *Macy's Thanksgiving Parade,* marching right down New York's Fifth Avenue. But none of that materialized because no one in the band, except me, was interested in taking their music career to the next level, turning professional, finding gigs, and believe me, their parents could care even less. All that mattered in Garden City was going to the right college, getting a good corporate job and, for the girls at least, not getting pregnant before you had that wedding ring on your finger. Me, I could have cared less about college and still think a college degree is one of the most overpriced objects still for sale in the USA.[20] Each to their own, but I never looked back ... well hardly ever.

By 1967, my hair was long, I was listening to *Paul Butterfield's Blues Band*, reading Sonny Glover's *Blues Harp* instruction book and trying to score *pot*, which is what we called marijuana back then. Times were changing and me with them. The blues seemed to suit me for obvious reasons, it's the music that celebrates *loss*. In fact, you could say I've had the blues one way or another ever since 1965. When I was a senior in High School, a new kid moved into Garden City from Chicago, a musician, who knew all about the blues and beyond, even knowing a song by the 13th *Floor Elevators*, real psychedelic stuff, that I had never heard of. For a while I traded him my *Gibson J-160E* Acoustic guitar for his white *Fender Telecaster*, putting a banjo string on top so I could bend those notes way across the neck of the guitar, up on the 12th fret and beyond, like lead guitarist Mike Bloomfield[21] was doing effortlessly. In the fall of 1966, I finally scored a *nickel bag* of marijuana from an older musician I knew, an organ player who had backed Bo Diddly, and me and bandmate Tommy Tucker sat in a parking lot in Hempstead and rolled our first joint and my drug history began right then and there. There was a talent contest at my high school and we entered with a psychedelic version of *The Rapscallions*, all of us now with long hair, stovepipe pants and paisley *Tom Jones* shirts, singing *You're Gonna Miss Me*[22]. Before we were even finished the principal pulled the electric plug on us, but I didn't care; in fact, that was even better for my growing notoriety. By then, I was one of a handful in my class who smoked pot, knew who Ken Kesey and his Merry Pranksters were, and listened to Miles Davis *Kind of Blue* on the library record player. I now had a steady and very cool girlfriend, Laura, who called me *Jimbo* and was driving me to school every morning in her tan *Mustang* coupe. Like so many baby boomer guys, I changed my style from surfer to hippie as the vibes changed around me, at a speed never before witnessed in generations. The Vietnam war was raging, and I wanted no part of it; let them send the old men who started the cold war into battle, hand a uniform and rifle to LBJ or Nixon and then see how fast peace would arrive. At least, that's how I always saw it. Still do, in fact ...

In the spring of 1967, my next band, *The King James Version* was playing a steady gig at the *305 Lounge*[23] in Hempstead and I sang just one number – *Like A Rolling Stone* – a portent of things to come. One night I sat in the parking lot behind the club in a friend's white Lincoln Continental and smoked something called DMT, the "instant coffee" version of psychedelic drugs. Next thing I knew the very stars above me seemed to be pummeling through the windshield of that car as infinity pulled me through the cosmos at the speed of light and I was freaking out big time. I eventually came down and even tried DMT a second and third time but some weeks later I was overcome with anxiety and one afternoon I went to see the Lee Marvin war flick *The Dirty Dozen* in the Roosevelt Field Cinema. There was a tough scene to watch in which a young soldier was being executed for murder and I swear I felt that noose tighten around my own neck. I bolted out of that movie theater and couldn't stop running or crying – my psyche had completely broken down. Next day, my mother sent me to a psychiatrist who was the son of the same shrink that had treated her when she had a nervous breakdown and he immediately prescribed me *Thorazine* and a newly available anti-depressant, *Aventyl*. Honestly, I don't know if these powerful drugs made me feel better or worse, but I stayed in bed for weeks, overcome with a nameless dread, only gradually being able to take short summer drives with my mother in her car. To this day, I don't really know what happened, my shrink said it was the DMT that kicked off a *post-traumatic* reaction to seeing my father die and the ensuing panic of not being able to do anything to help him or prevent his death. I might have been spared the horrors of Vietnam, but I still have PTSD[24] like so many returning vets of that war and the many that have followed.

If there was an upside to my breakdown it was that I stopped taking drugs for a while because pot made me paranoid and I began taking summer classes at nearby *Nassau Community College*, studying music, literature and acting, with an academic vigor I didn't know I possessed. That next fall semester, armed with excellent grades, I got admitted as a full-time student. For the time being, at least, I was safe from being sent to the jungles of southeast Asia. Some years later, when my time at NCC was through, the same psychiatrist who treated me for PTSD wrote a letter to my draft board stating that while under his care, I suffered from *spells of disorientation* and the army, probably imagining that I might get confused as to where to point my rifle in a moment of such disorientation, granted me a medical deferment. The day I received that notice in the mail was one of the best days of my life and the first person I told about it was a pretty blond girl from my brother's class, Geraldine, who was working at the local Pizza shop where I stopped in to have a slice to celebrate. She didn't make me pay for my pizza and five years later I would marry her. Like I said, I saw my future before it saw me.

MY MOTHER, JOSEPHINE, WAS BORN IN ST. PETERSBURG, Florida in 1926, but grew up on Long Island in Baldwin, once a small village on the south shore, now just part of the suburban sprawl that never seems to end in that part of the world. The working farms that were there when she was a girl have long since been replaced by shopping malls and housing developments. When her father was eight years old and walking home from school in Tupelo, Mississippi, a boy who worked on his family's cotton farm shouted out to him that his mother had just died. James K. Wilson dropped his books and ran home in a panic, finding his mother gone from ovarian cancer that morning, I believe. My mother thinks he never got over the shock and terror of that day. Maybe he had PTSD like me. He's the only alcoholic before me in the family that I can identify with any certainty. Apparently, Papa Wilson stopped drinking well into his sixties, when his ulcers became too painful to bear. But for years before that my mother, then a young teenager, would accompany her own mother to the Baldwin Long Island Railroad train station, both of them hoping he would step down from the eastbound train, returning home with the other commuters after putting in his working day as an insurance agent in Brooklyn. Too many evenings they would wait in vain and my grandfather would finally show up hours or even days later, drunk after a binge of alcohol. My grandmother would put him to bed and try her best to hide it all from the neighbors. My grandfather had a brother, actually named *Happy*, who died young from alcoholism and another who was a prominent general in the US Army and National Guard and was on duty when James Meredith integrated Ol' Miss University in 1962. My grandfather, who we called *Papa* for some reason, was a lifelong Democrat who hardly approved of fellow *Tupelo son* Elvis Presley, figuring he must be a decent young man and *a good old boy*, because he shared his fine house with his parents once he made it big.

Of all my relatives, Papa Wilson was my favorite. I loved his homey southern accent, the way he let us grandkids dress up in his scratchy wool WWI army uniform and *dough boy* helmet, and how he'd skillfully throw the baseball around with us in the backyard of his simple Baldwin, Long Island house. He also liked to take his grandchildren for leisurely walks down to the *creek,* part of the *South Bay* estuary, at the end of Arlington Avenue where he and my grandmother lived and where my mother and her sister, Aunt Jean, had been brought up. We walked on the creaky wooden docks and fished for soft-shelled crabs or *snappers*[25] in late July and August and to me, who had just discovered Mark Twain, it was almost like being on the

Mississippi River and I dreamed of being on a raft with Huck Finn and following the current to ... I don't know, maybe Freeport, the next town over? That was the thing that bothered me about Long Island, I had a sense of being trapped there; it jutted out from Manhattan like a giant fish and there was no way to get off it without crossing above, below or through water. But my grandfather must have liked Long Island because he stayed there as long as he could, until he was moved to a nursing home in New Jersey in his eighties and I never once recall him saying he missed Mississippi. I've never visited Tupelo myself but it's on my bucket list and my sister Michelle, far more of a family historian then I, has and she was surprised to see that so many of our southern relatives there seemed to have *drink holders* mounted in their car, where they could place their cocktails, called *shooters,* which I suppose is a derivative of *shots.* It reminds me of the way John Wayne would march right up to the saloon bar in so many westerns, gruffly ordering a bottle of whiskey before punching a few guys out and drowning his sorrows with shot glasses full to the brim of *rotgut* when something, usually a woman, was troubling him. When I was ten and started getting a weekly allowance, I went down to *Lamstons,* the local *Five & Ten* cents variety shop down the block and bought my own shot glass and filled it with tea while I dressed up with my toy guns, playing Jesse James. My grandmother, Ruth Wilson, claimed that a distant relative actually heard the shot that killed him in 1882 while living in St. Joseph, Missouri. By the time I heard about it, my grandfather's alcoholism had become part of the family lore. He was an old man by then and his drinking days were behind him while mine were just beginning. There's a song of mine, *Chain of Pain,* where I tried to place addiction and alcoholism in a generational context:

Chain of Pain – coming at you like a train – each generation - always the same.

And like the Jimi Hendrix song says, I hear my train a coming...

My maternal grandmother, Ruth Dewey Wilson, was born and raised in Flemington, New Jersey. She came from solid middle-class roots and her family could trace their origins to the boat that followed the *Mayflower* to Plymouth Rock in the 17th century. Her father served as the mayor of Flemington for many years and her great uncle, Admiral George Dewey, was the naval hero of the Spanish-American War who *liberated* the Philippines from the Spanish at the Battle of Manila ... and made it a *de facto* U.S. colony! When Admiral Dewey returned triumphantly to the U.S. in 1899, President McKinley presented him with an elaborate jewel-encrusted sword in a grand ceremony under the Capitol rotunda in Washington DC. The sword had been custom-made by *Tiffany & Co.*, the famous jewelry store where my mother, nearly a century later, would work day in and day out until her retirement at age sixty-five, selling fine china on 57th Street and 5th Avenue. She hated working there, but in all fairness, she hated working anywhere. Unlike her husband, my grandmother was a lifelong Republican and devout Methodist[26] who absolutely hated both Jayne Mansfield[27] and Arthur Godfrey[28]. I don't know what my grandmother thought about Elvis, but she was always kind to her grandchildren and said her mantra, "Bless your little heart!" on as many occasions as possible. She also had a bound collection of Shakespeare's plays high on her bookshelf that I started to pour through as soon as I was tall enough to reach them.

My actress wife Françoise believes I'm a rock 'n roll version of *Hamlet* and the history of my father, my mother and my stepfather does fit a similar scenario somewhat. I was sixteen at the time of my father's fatal heart attack, it happened in the middle of the night, but I was still awake, sitting at my desk, doing what, I don't remember, maybe playing guitar or writing a short story or reading *East of Eden*. I only remember my mother bursting into my room in a panic, *Your father is having some kind of attack!* I followed her back to their bedroom where my father was lying in bed, sitting up, his arms lifted up at his sides with his elbows jutting out, gasping for breath and fighting for his life. I don't know if he was even aware of my presence in the room, his eldest son standing in front of him, my eyes struck wide with terror. In fact, I don't know if he was seeing anything at all at that point. Then my father suddenly stopped breathing and his eyes rolled back up in his head. There was a terrible moment of silence and then a sound came from deep in his throat, the *death rattle,* and he was frozen in time, lost to all of us who loved him forever and ever.

My mother got on the phone to call the police, the fire department, *anyone* and sent me across the street to get help. I ran as fast as I could down 10th Street to the house of Dr. Kanner, our next door neighbor and pounded on his door. Dressed in his pajamas, the doctor soon came down and I beseeched him to hurry, my father was dying, and he understood, saying he had to get his medical bag first and hurriedly went back up his stairs. I dropped to my knees on his front stoop and prayed with a faith I didn't really possess or understand; *Please God don't let my father die! Please God!* Together, Dr. Kanner and I hurried back to my house and ran up the stairs. He asked my mother and I to wait outside while he went into their bedroom alone. We stood outside the bedroom door and the doctor emerged just a few minutes later, a shocked and sorrowful look on his face and said, *I'm sorry, he's gone.* My mother and I collapsed into each other's arms in grief. Neither of our lives would ever be the same again. I can say that when I lost my father, I lost whatever faith I had and it was only after the birth of my son Gaspard, when I was forty, that it has returned in bits and pieces. I have thought of my father and that night nearly every day since, even though it happened over fifty years ago, and I miss him even more the older I get. As Hamlet said, *He was a man. I shall not look upon his like again.* And I never have.

My father had an older brother, Arthur Arthurs, who had changed his last name from Murphy so as not to appear Irish as all his friends and wife were Jewish. Arthur was my proverbial *rich Uncle,* who owned a very profitable huge automobile dealership, *Paramount Oldsmobile* in Brooklyn, and had been an early investor in the *Miracle Mile,* an upscale shopping center in Manhasset, pioneering that sort of consumer paradise. Arthur lived with his wife and two children in Kings Point, an exclusive area of Great Neck, in a modern house on a cliff with a tall flagpole in the yard, overlooking Long Island Sound. The lights of the newly constructed *Throngs Neck Bridge*, gracefully arched like a diamond necklace, twinkled in the distance. Arthur had a telescope mounted on a tri-pod in his den whose large *picture* windows allowed us to gaze over the *Long Island Sound*, and he liked to show us the sights through its powerful lenses, the bridge, the colonial buildings of the Merchant Marine Academy next store, the Manhattan skyline in the distance. We visited there often because he and my father were very close and apparently in business together. My mother disputes all of that now and does not have nice things to say about him, but Arthur's name was listed on many *Aquashow* programs as *executive producer*. Some few years after losing his brother, *my father*, my Uncle Arthur also lost his young son Kevin in a tragic and freak accident on a winter's day when the boy was shoveling snow in the driveway. Arthur had allowed Kevin to start up his car that was parked there and sit inside to get warm but apparently snow had backed up into the exhaust pipe and Kevin was overcome with carbon dioxide fumes. We got the news from Gus, one of my Uncle's employees at the car dealership, and our whole family drove into the city to see Arthur and his wife, my Aunt Betty. I remember walking into that apartment where his daughter Joan lived with her husband, songwriter Wes Farrel, and he was sitting alone in a darkened room. I've never seen a sadder man in all my life and the image of him there, completely devastated, still haunts me. In the space of five years he had lost his mother, his brother and now his son. My uncle Arthur died suddenly a few years later of a heart attack himself, only in his mid-fifties, while vacationing in West Hampton and after that we lost all contact with that side of the family, not even aware when my Aunt Betty took her own life until years after it happened.

    My father had not died at a good time, but when is a good time to die when you have three kids and a young wife? Apparently, after many boom years his restaurant was not doing well, something had changed in the IRS expense account deduction allowance and business dinners and lunches were way down. At least that was the story I heard but I was only sixteen and into surfing and girls so what did I know? I *do* know that nine months after his death my family were forced to move from our 10th Street mansion, where a scenic wall shielded our property from the leafy street in front of it, to a grim corner house in the modest section of town where the skinny trees looked like they were planted yesterday in contrast to the stately old oaks I use to climb in our backyard. In fact, during the week after my father died, I took an ax from the tool shed and cut down one of our trees. Papa Wilson stood by and watched, smoking a cigarette, as I swung that ax in a rage until that small tree, a tree probably close to my own age, had fallen. I'm not sure what drove me to do that, but it was an impulse I could not deny and my grandfather seemed to understand where it came from, maybe he had felt something similar when his mother passed away when he was a young boy. Of all the things that happened in our family for the ritual of death, tearful visits from family friend, solemn funerals, a dismal burial in an immense cemetery, chopping down that tree was the only thing that made sense to me.

Strangely, I don't remember anything about that move at all. I've blocked it out completely and it's like I went to sleep in one house and woke up in another. We sold my father's custom *Cadillac Fleetwood*, resigned from the *Cherry Valley Country Club* and stopped going out to restaurants. I'd prefer not to re-live any of those tragic days and dismal years if I could avoid it. But I can't because it's so much the reason I am who I am, that I do what I do. Jay Gatsby[29] might have believed you can change the past but I have no such illusions. Whether you're a songwriter or an author, our past is the iron ore we make steel from; or, as I wrote ten years later in my song *Deco Dance - the past is the only thing that lasts if you move too fast...*

If this was a rock *bio flick* and not a written biography, you would now see me larger than life, standing next to Bruce Springsteen, in full color on a huge screen, both of us on the stage of *Stade de France* in Paris. It's 2016, and I'm standing on that stage with my son Gaspard, our guitars still strapped on, having just performed *Born to Run* with *Bruce Springsteen and the E-Street Band,* in front of 80,000 fans. Then the camera would pan overhead, and you would see a jet plane passing through clouds, and the roar of that crowd would be replaced by the roar of jet engines. *Fade out* from 2016 and *fade in* to 1971 and you would see a wide-eyed twenty-two-year-old American with long blond hair and bell bottom jeans, putting on his *Ray-Ban* aviator shades as he walks off a Boeing 707 at Amsterdam's Schiphol airport, guitar in hand, rock dreams in head. That boy was me and if you're looking for my *Rosebud*[30], that *Pan Am* jet is a good candidate.

Chapter Two

"YOUNG BOY STAND HERE" - FEDERICO FELLINI

Elliott & Matthew Murphy in a scene from Federico Fellini's "Roma"

My 1971 European odyssey, six years after my father's death, was my *metamorphosis,* a brief but crucial phase which changed my future, and the ramifications of those months I spent in Europe at that time probably have much to do with why I chose to eventually live in Paris, why my wife *Françoise* is French, why my son Gaspard was born here. I believe that I am an ex-patriate by my very nature, someone who *feels more at home when they are not at home*. Make no mistake, I love my country as much as the next honest guy (or gal) but I've travelled so far and so wide that I can't condemn all other residents of this planet for the sin of not being American. I always liked the term *international,* there's some ingrained excitement to it, a certain flair to it, an alluring promise of exotic locales but I didn't desert the USA – it was more a case of the USA deserting me. And who knows? Maybe I'll move back some day. *Venice Beach* has always appealed to me as a cool spot to retire to ...

Back to 1971, thanks to my beautiful older sister Michelle, a fabled *Pan Am* stewardess, I was entitled to a steep family discount on trans-Atlantic flight tickets and as there was little else going on in my life at the time, I chose to go to ... Amsterdam. Why Amsterdam? Because to a long-haired, pot smoking, East Coast hipster, Amsterdam was the obvious destination. That still-quant town, with its picturesque canals and *Rijksmuseum* full of dark Rembrandt paintings, was overflowing with *freaks* because of it's well-known tolerance for soft-drugs. You could say that the Netherlands was way ahead of its time when you consider the current momentum for the legalization of marijuana in so many US states today. What we are experiencing is the *Amsterdaming* of the western world! Ironically, this long-overdue *embracement* of the legalization of pot has arrived much too late to interest me at all, as drugs and I got a divorce a very long time ago and I have no desire to get back together. But that wasn't always the case and in 1971 Amsterdam was the European version of what San Francisco must have been like during the *Summer of Love* four years earlier, plus the added attraction of having the safest, almost quant, *red-light district* you're ever going to find, where prostitutes, dressed in lingerie and leather, tapped their keys on their windows to lure you inside. Hippies, counter-culture misfits, and stoners from all over the world, flooded Amsterdam, camping out in *Vondelpark* where grams of hashish served as the local currency. Clubs such as the *Paradiso* presented top touring bands from the UK and beyond and *Melkweg* was a late-night venue where you could dance by yourself for hours, stoned out of your mind on Afghani hashish, and nobody would look at you askance. I can still vividly recall the liberating sensation I felt when I disembarked at *Schiphol Airport*; how this tremendous psychic burden was all at once lifted from my shoulders and I started to feel something close to *joy,* bordering on *freedom,* for the first time since I had seen my father die six years before. My step-father Slim's abuse, my mother's battle with depression, all of this and more was miraculously left back home on the flatlands of Long Island, on another continent in a different time zone, that I was in no hurry to return to. Most significantly, I also decided at some point during my first *old world* voyage, that I would finally and forever take my given name *Elliott* as my own. On my birth certificate it might say *Elliott James Murphy Jr.,* but to spare the redundancy of having two *Elliott* around the house, my family had always called me *Jimmy,* the shortened version of my middle name James. But when I briefly returned from Europe for Christmas in 1971, after six months away, it was only as Elliott Murphy. Like my father, Jimmy was dead.

After spending sufficient time in Amsterdam to learn how to properly mix hashish with *Drum* tobacco in the palm of your hand and then light it up in a *chillum* pipe with a piece of cloth wrapped around to cool the smoke, I travelled on a wide continental arc beginning at Amsterdam's *Centraal Station*, to Brussels' *Gare de Midi*, then Paris' *Gare du Nord* and, finally Rome's *Stazione Termini* via the stylish European trains of the time with provocative names like *Le Train Blue* (The Blue Train) or *Fleche d'Or* (Golden Arrow). What a difference from the totally un-romantic *Long Island Rail Road* commuter line back home. The *Termini* railway station in Rome was aptly titled, because once I arrived in the *Eternal City*, it would be where I spent the bulk of my European journey, busking with a guitar on the terraces of *Piazza Navona* and landing what I euphemistically call a *bit part* in Federico Fellini's film *Fellini Roma,* where I was able to chat with writer Gore Vidal and Andy Warhol film star Donyale Luna, as we patiently waited for the *maestro* to set up the day's shot. The golden age of Italian cinema might have been entering its crepuscule but thanks to filmmakers such as Fellini and Luchino Visconti, Rome was still drawing movie stars and well-known filmmakers from all over the world. I had casting sessions with some top directors including *Hard Days Night's* Richard Lester, and briefly hung out with actor Dennis Christopher who found fame in the 1979 bicycle racing film *Breaking Away.* More memorably, I had leap-frog affairs with Elisabeth and Justine, two lovely Swedish blonds, an untenable situation where I just couldn't decide between the two. *Hershey Bar* size bars of hashish were hidden on the roof of our *Campo Di Fiori* hotel, just outside the communal toilet; where we lived in constant anxiety of a *Carabinieri* bust, as drugs, even marijuana, were highly illegal in Italy and unlike Amsterdam, garnished long prison sentences. Well-known French actor, Pierre Clémenti, served seventeen months in an Italian prison for a minor drug offense and we lived in fear of the same fate coming our way. But that was not to be my destiny. Never been arrested for drugs (or anything else) and have faith that I never will be. Unlike Jim Morrison, Mick Jagger and a host of other musicians, you will find no police photos of me holding a small sign with my height, weight and age and arrest number if you search on *Google*. Even if such notoriety can prove to be a smart career move …

During my stay at *Nassau Community College* in 1968-70, I had studied acting and even garnered high marks for a monologue taken from Edward Albee's play *Zoo Story,* but I knew in my heart that movie acting wasn't for me, although that seemed to be what everyone was doing in Rome at that time; all the *beautiful people* lounging around cafes in Piazza Navona, sipping Cappuccino while going on occasional casting calls. I had travelled to Europe with my Garden City buddy Rory Calhoun who'd been here before and knew his way around all the major cities. One of the reasons we called

Rome home base was that Rory's brother was living there with Farley Granger, a well-known American actor who had starred in Alfred Hitchcock's classic suspense film *Stranger on a Train*, the story of two complete strangers who meet on a train and agree to engage in a murderous conspiracy, with disastrous repercussions. It will make you think twice about that person on your next flight who starts up an uninvited conversation with you. Many years later I wrote a song with the same title but a different plot that began, *What was I doing – I must have been mad ...*

Farley Granger was the first genuine Hollywood movie star I ever met. Tall and handsome with a friendly smile, glistening white teeth, perfectly tanned, black wavy hair and stretched out in a deck chair on the terrace of their Roman penthouse, dressed in a plush white terrycloth bathrobe. He and his partner, Bob Calhoun, were also the first openly gay couple, living in apparent harmony, that I had ever met before. They were both so welcoming, so down to earth, yet so sophisticated and extremely helpful to me that I was ashamed about how back in high school *jocks* taunted any effeminate and perhaps gay boy who walked the school hallways. I never insulted nor teased anyone myself but neither did I stand up to defend those who became the butt of cruel jokes. I was a product of my environment, like everyone else, and it took this European adventure to open my eyes and realize how provincial my Garden City upbringing really had been and how my values, no matter how cool I thought I was, needed an overhaul. We followed Farley and Bob to the island of Ponza (most beautiful beaches I ever swam in) and Rory and I and another friend camped out on the beach in a tent while smoking opium under the hot sun. Through Farley and Bob, I met a sophisticated, Italian married couple whose name I remember as Johnny and Laura with a beach house on Ponza and who owned a posh disco back in Rome, *Scacca Motto* near Piazza del Popolo. One night over dinner, Johnny proposed to hire me as the new DJ of the club. *Why me?* I asked. Well, he thought I had a great look, long blond hair, twenty-eight-inch waist, and it would be great for the image of the place which needed ... something new. They both searched for the appropriate term, *To help us get more with it ... and you look like a hippy ... not dirty of course!* said Laura. *And with multo... steel!* Added Johnny. *Stile?* I asked. *Like iron?* His wife corrected him, *Style!* She corrected. A paid gig playing records while watching a bevy of beautiful Italian babes shimmy around the dance floor? it sounded good to me.

Of course, even though I'd never done that job before, never spun a record on a turntable for money, I agreed. But because I was a hip rock 'n roll musician, I was under the arrogant notion that my job was like a radio DJ, to musically *educate* the disco's patrons, show them what's really cool to dance to. When I arrived at the DJ booth the first night I found the record selection, to my amazement, to be almost entirely obscure R&B, and the only name I recognized was *James Brown*, no kidding. I asked a waiter if there were any more records and he pointed me toward the cave where the wine was stocked. I discovered a huge pile of albums and I brought those that appealed to me back to the DJ booth, mostly *Motown, Stax* and *Rolling Stones* records. But when I started playing that stuff nobody seemed to know how to move to it. No matter what I put on, The Stones' *Brown Sugar* or the Four Tops' *Reach Out I'll Be There,* the dance floor was deserted. This was not good because as dancing made the patrons of the disco thirsty and sitting glaring at me did not I was ruining business. Also, as I had *carte blanche* at the bar, I was making up for the lack of drinks being served by drinking way too much myself and on my third night I accidentally knocked into the turntable and send the needle scratching along the surface of *Sex Machine Part II.* It was like everyone in the place froze and stared at me until I nervously got a record spinning again. Within a few weeks I was replaced with a professional DJ, who played James Brown and little else, and kept everyone feeling like they were great dancers. The couple who owned the place were very cool and shrugged their shoulders, *Que Sera, Sera* gave me an envelope full of *Lira.*

Sometime later, Farley Granger had another suggestion - that I go

Just A Story from America

out to *CineCitta* and try to get hired as an extra in a western film as I knew how to ride horses. It's a crazy long story as to what happened next but most importantly, my brother Matthew had come to Rome to visit me and my friend Rory, who had managed to ship his 1200cc *Harley Davidson* to Italy, retreated back to the US for a while, not sure why. So in his absence, Matthew and I got on that huge *Harley* and drove out to *CineCitta* studios, explaining that we were American cowboy actors and probably through some misunderstanding, were led to an office on the studio lot and told to sit down in a room and wait. Which is exactly what we did until a short time later, director Federico Fellini himself opened the door, said *Ciao* and then shut the door. We continued to wait until his assistant came back in to tell us we were hired for a week's work and to come back on Monday at 8am sharp for makeup.

Federico Fellini was in the midst of shooting *Roma,* his sprawling *paean* to the *eternal city,* and for the next week we moved all over town for various shots. As you might expect, my best scenes ended up on the cutting room floor but a small yet significant piece of my *mythology*, admittedly of very short duration, remains in the finished film where Matthew and I were caught on camera in a crowd scene, almost a riot, following a boxing match. I was positioned to lead the action and Fellini himself stood in front of me, put his hand on my shoulder and said, "Young boy, you stand here." Those five words, were probably a totally inconsequential act for him but to me it was nothing less than monumental. I can still hear his voice ...

Many, many years later, in 1991,I was playing a solo gig at a historic jazz and blues club, *Big Mama* located in *Trastevere,* on the west bank of the Tiber. I told the story of my moment of glory in *Roma* to the audience and after the show, an Italian journalist approached to say he actually had Federico Fellini's address if I ever wanted to contact him. And so, I wrote to him, and sent him my latest CD too, telling him how grateful I was for having played in *Roma,* how I would never forget meeting him, and on and on. A week later, after I returned to Paris, while checking my mailbox, I discovered to my utter astonishment a letter with an Italian stamp, addressed to me, and when I turned it over, on the other side of the envelope was written *Federico Fellini* and his Rome return address. Fellini's letter was written by hand in English but with many errors and some words crossed out and others added in. This is what the *maestro* said to me:

Thank you for your sweet letter dear Elliott. I would like to tell you that I remember perfectly your incisive [sic] performance in Roma as all the critics have remarked, unfortunately the years have weakened my memory. Anyway, I really liked what you wrote me. I will try to listen to your record. I sincerely wish you good work and good luck. With friendship, Federico Fellini.

Within a year of that letter, in 1992, Federico Fellini was dead and the next time I went back to Rome it felt like a different city to me, much the same as New York seemed to lose some undefined artistic *edginess* after Andy Warhol died. I walked all night, revisiting many of the places where *Roma* had been filmed and, by dawn, a song started coming to me, all six verses, complete in an hour or less; almost like I was channeling some spirit as I struggled to write the words down fast enough before more came tumbling out of my thoughts. I had six solid verses and the song's title could only be *Is Fellini really dead*:

Nights like this are a luxury there are five stars are overhead - the rhythm of the footsteps some they follow me although I feel led - me I'm standing perfectly still and just holding my breath and wondering if Rome exists after Fellini's death...

In spite of my brief and incandescent experience working with one of the greatest film directors of our time, I still knew that acting was not for me, at least not yet. Too much waiting time, not enough applause and, most importantly, once in Europe I had started to write songs like I had never written before, serious, good songs or so I believed, with a focused intention that was new to me. Suddenly, I had a sense that my life was about to change, as if I was finally standing in the right line, just waiting for destiny to take me aboard its magic bus and I better have my ticket ready. And my ticket would be my songs.

∼

I HAD TRIED MY HAND AT SONGWRITING IN MY LAST LONG Island band, a heavy rock outfit called *Bang-Zoom*[1] and one of those songs *Marilyn*[2] even made it onto my first album *Aquashow*, but my European *sojourn* had unleashed an even more powerful muse then the *Marshall* Amps that powered my lengthy guitar solos. I discovered a passion and intensity for putting words to music that must have been there all this time, hiding behind my pain and joy, and songs such as *Last of the Rock Stars* (about my rock star dreams), *How's the Family* (inspired by my shattered family) and *White Middle Class Blues* (about the Long Island suburbia I didn't want to go back to) soon were born. As my French poet friend Michel Bulteau says, *when the demons are summoned, they will always appear,* and I was soon making my demons dance to melody, rhyme and rhythm with a little harmonica thrown in for *Dylanesque* color. If there is a cycle to the bewildering lives we live, and if rebirth is a part of that cycle, then I can say that the artist in me was born the night my father died and that artist came of age during that European trip. From the ashes rises the Phoenix ...

While still in Amsterdam, I had bought two bootleg songbooks from an Irish guy selling records in Dam Square, companion pieces to many of the anonymous bootleg records that were just starting to pop-up on the scene; one was full of all the *Rolling Stones* songs up until that time and the other, the same for Bob Dylan. I consumed both with a religious fervor: my two testament bibles with no commandments, maybe a hundred songs or more. My friend Rory had brought with him a nice *Martin* acoustic guitar, never sure why he even owned it as he didn't play, but lucky for me because reverently, I started to figure out the chords to many of the songs inside those two books, like a *hands-on* course in rock and folk songwriting, and I still play both the Stones' *Wild Horses* and Dylan's *I Want You* to this day, reminders of the hours I spent in my room at the *Hotel Brouwer* in Amsterdam trying to figure them out. When I busked on the streets of Rome that first trip, I never made much money but on my next time over to Europe, while staying in Switzerland I met a local guy who really knew the ropes about busking. His advice was simple: don't play long, pass the hat quickly and get out; that way you stay cool with the café owners. I did just that for a few weeks while waiting for my now girlfriend Geraldine to bust out of her private all girls finishing school, located on the shore of *Lac Leman* ...

Chapter Three

LET ME TELL YOU ABOUT A GIRL I KNOW ...

Elliott Murphy performing at the Wine Bar open mic night in San Francisco 1972

*G*eraldine was wife number one, my Zelda, my cheerleader, my partner in crime and a fashion icon in her own way; a once beloved companion in a doomed and still fabled marriage for those who witnessed it go down in flames. Or snorted up a straw...

A beautiful and smart blond, from one of the wealthier Garden City families, Geraldine grew up in a fine house on 11th Street and from her back yard you could see the house on 10th Street where I saw my father die on the worst day of my life. How strange is that? Geraldine and I already shared some history as I had taken her out on a date when she was just sixteen years before doing an about face and dating her best friend Cynthia, a statuesque ballet dancer, who was just a little bit wilder. Geraldine dropped off my radar until I came back from Europe the first time during Christmas 1971, and while *bivouacked* at my friend Curtis Knapp's house at a three-day non-stop party, we rediscovered each other. We left that party joined at the hip or someplace anatomically not too far away. Instant soul-mates, we had both drank the *Kool-Aid*[1] and were fully invested in a mutually shared belief that we were setting out on a pre-destined *cosmic* journey together. Like me, Geraldine was in the grips of *rock 'n roll dreams*, having already dated a semi-rock star drummer and hanging out briefly with Beatle George Harrison and, needless to say, found that the lifestyle suited her well, best described by the *sage of the rock age,* Keith Richards, as *getting wasted elegantly.* We imagined ourselves as real-life characters from the film *Performance,* passing leisurely days soaking in bubble baths, illuminated by a burning chorus of candles and surrounded by racks upon racks of exotic clothes, long silk scarves and colorful Moroccan vests, all fueled by whatever substance might be *apropos* to the mood of the moment. A kind of Mick Jagger and Anita Pallenberg[2] style in the film *Performane.* The wake-up call came when Geraldine's parents, envisioning disaster coming their virtuous daughter's way after her brief time of hanging with rock royalty when she disappeared from the house for days on end, knew that something must be done and quick. Thus, they had planned, and paid, for her to spend a year in one of those elite *finishing schools* that dot the tranquil shores of Lac Leman, Switzerland. Geraldine left for Europe just days after we left the party, where we had *pledged our trough* to the strains of The Stones *Let It Bleed*. Not long after, like Lancelot, I followed her, both of us planning our great escape all the while.

Her school was located just down the lake from Montreux, a gorgeous Swiss town, renowned for both the *Montreux Jazz Festival* (which I played in 1983) and that author Vladimir Nabokov had written his novels there while living in the five-star *Montreux Palace Hotel*. I don't know if they taught Nabokov in Geraldine's all-girls finishing school, but I can say that the *Lolita* spirit was alive and well in the dorms. When Geraldine sent me a few Polaroids of her and her teen roommates posing topless with a shared *come-hither* expression I bought a plane ticket for Geneva *tout suite*. And as Nabokov himself once wrote, ... *the rest is rust and stardust.*

My first impression of Geraldine's school was that most of the *students* were the wild teenage daughters of wealthy South American or Asian families and the schools' job was merely to guarantee that their daughters' virginity would remain intact while their education was given the *finishing* touch. In this incongruous setting, this flock of *Lolitas,* as revved-up and ready to go as the baby swans paddling madly on the lake-front, were allowed out daily for one brief hour unchaperoned. While waiting impatiently for Geraldine's daily visits, I stayed in a cheap two-star hotel further up the hill from the lake which stank of fresh paint; writing songs and short stories, and, in spite of my dreary accommodations, dreaming big. Nights, I would take the train to Lausanne and busk in the smoky cafés in the old town, where I found the Swiss to be very generous if you didn't play too long or loud, as my newfound *manager* had suggested. But finally, Geraldine had enough of learning which fork to use for what dish, and we decided to bust her out of that school under the cover of moonlight, literally throwing all her clothing out of her second story dormitory window and scurrying off, like thieves in the night, taking the ferryboat to Geneva and finally a long flight to San Francisco via London. We were on the move, heading to that unknown destination, to that place *where we really want to go*[3] Not much time to soak in a bubble bath with me carrying both an *Olivetti* portable typewriter and an *Epiphone Frontier* acoustic guitar; we were somewhere between Scott & Zelda and Mick & Anita, I would like to think euphemistically, of course.

Summer of 1971 in laid back San Francisco, we shared an apartment on *California Street* with a girl whose name I forget but whom I clearly remember working nights as a topless pole dancer while rehearsing her moves at home during the day without the aid of pole or clothing. We seemed to subsist on little else but *Tapioca* pudding, which was cheap, filling and the only thing we knew how to cook. Geraldine was already familiar with those hilly city streets, climbed by picturesque cable cars, having run away once before to Haight Ashbury[4] when she was just out of high school. During her first brief time there, she had worked for Werner Erhardt (who later invented *EST* - Erhardt Seminar Training) and sold encyclopedias and cookbooks for him door to door. When I met him, Erhardt seemed like a charismatic character indeed, who would have made the perfect rock manager, but *EST* was too close to *Scientology* for my taste and it all smelled like a scam and a cult where those at the top got all the goodies while the pawns at the bottom felt guilty for, well, not being on the top. Anyway, I instinctively backed away from it, never being much of a *joiner* anyway and when some of Geraldine's old *EST* buddies came by to visit and took note of my obvious lack of enthusiasm for their new-age *ponzi scheme*, they took Geraldine aside and told her she better get rid of me, pronto, if she wanted to get *clear*. But how could they know that Geraldine, like me, had succumbed to the only cult that suited our wardrobe and sleeping habits: *Rock 'n Roll*.

We'd lounge around the apartment during the day, me writing songs, and come dark I would venture out to play *open mic* nights at the wine bars and cafés down by *Fisherman's Wharf*, all the while hoping to find the perfect manager, my own Brian Epstein, because the number one rule of show business is *you can't promote yourself, baby, no matter how good you are.* I finally did find a manager, or at least kind of, in another Garden City guy, Mark Russo, who was mainly a photographer and took rolls and rolls of film of Geraldine and I on the streets of San Francisco that I still have; we look hungry, slightly exotic and both bored and bound for glory. Marc conveniently lived in the same California Street building as us; the place a somewhat frayed reminder of *The Summer of Love*, its exterior painted in different hews of psychedelic mellow yellows and marine blues with a definite *Magical Mystery Tour* vibe. Rumor was that musician Steve Stills owned the building although, to my recollection, he never dropped by to personally pick up the rent. When I sat down and played my original songs to Marc he all at once became a true believer, going so far as to use his own funds to fly down to Los Angeles, and play my demo tape for any *A&R*[5] folks who would let him in their door. Marc tried his best to get me a record deal, to hype up some interest and I remember that he got a very positive response from now defunct *Playboy Records* who wanted to see me play live soon. But that never happened.

Memorial Day Weekend 1972, I landed a gig at a beer joint somewhere in the Bay area, over in Oakland I think, and the deal was they didn't pay you anything, but you could drink for free. So, I drank all the pitchers of *Coors* beer I could with many shots of *Jack Daniels* bourbon thrown down my gullet as well and the next day I awoke with a really mean hangover, worse than usual, that only got worse as they day progressed. Finally, forcing myself out of bed that evening, I got dressed and put on a canary yellow shirt that I had bought in Paris. When Geraldine saw me, her eyes widened, "Elliott, you're as yellow as that shirt!" Jaundiced indeed, I had contracted *Hepatitis A* but didn't know it until we went to *San Francisco General Hospital* and I was diagnosed by an intern, after he got through with all the stabbing and shooting victims being ambulanced in from the holiday weekend. Man, I was really sick! The sickest I had ever been in my life, with no means of getting better on my own. With my tail between my legs, I called my mother to rescue me and she arranged a plane ticket back to New York and nursed me back to health. God bless her for that – not the last time she would save my butt. On the drive home from *JFK airport* on the too familiar *Southern State Parkway,* back to Garden City, back to the little house I never wanted to set foot in again, I lay down in the back seat of that piss yellow *Maverick* as depressed as you can get at that age when you think your dreams have crashed and burned. I was twenty-two.

Once I recovered from *Hepatitis A,* and after Geraldine recovered from a harrowing illegal abortion that landed her in an emergency ward, her and I, accompanied by my brother Matthew, began nightly trips to the city, mostly hanging out at *Max's Kansas City,* which in 1970 was where the *Velvet Underground* had played their last series of concerts in a nine-week residence before Lou Reed had a nervous breakdown, quit the band and went back to Long Island to work for his father, an accountant. While in Rome, Andy Warhol *superstar* Donyale Luna had told me about *Max's* so I knew it was the happening place to go, to get discovered, to be noticed by New York's[6] *Avant Garde.* Both Lou Reed and I, at almost the same time, had retreated back to our family homes on Long Island at a crucial point in our lives, right before setting out to make a stand under the bright lights of Manhattan.

Chapter Four

AQUASHOW REBORN

Polydor Records: Matthew Murphy, Jerry Schoenbaum, Elliott Murphy, Peter Siegel 1972

I had missed seeing the *Velvet Underground* in the 1960's when Andy Warhol was both their patron and producer and they staged multi-media *Happenings* at *The Dom* disco on St.

Mark's Place, but once I got into the *Velvet's* 1971 album *Loaded*, containing *Sweet Jane, Rock and* Roll, *New Age* and other *sacred* songs, Lou Reed, although completely unbeknownst to him, became a songwriter role model, on an equal par with Bob Dylan and Jagger/Richards. Downtown hipsters spoke Lou's name in reverent tones but, as far as I knew, he had rarely made an appearance in New York City since his Long Island exile. I did briefly meet him following a Mitch Ryder show at the *Café au Go Go;* invited by Danny Fields, journalist, manager, record company executive and inveterate New York scene maker, who I had met at *Max's Kansas City.* There was a buzz that Lou might show up because Mitch Ryder had covered his anthem, *Rock and Roll,* with his fine band *Detroit* on his latest album. It was a courageous move on Mitch's part because even if Lou's name was highly venerated by the *Max's* crowd, for the most part he was still unknown in the rest of the country. For us locals, the *Velvet Underground* not only had an avant-garde reputation because of their connection with Warhol (Andy had *produced* their first album and even brought German model/singer *Nico* into the band) but also carried a menacing ambiance of sadomasochism and decadence due to songs such as *Venus in Furs* and *Heroin*. So, you can bet Lou Reed was an imposing figure for a 22-year-old nascent rocker to come face to face with. Thanks to my European sojourn, I had a certain hip *bona fide* going for me; I could throw around the right names and places, so when I saw Lou standing there, incongruously wearing a *Mickey Mouse* T-shirt and chatting amiably with Danny Fields, Danny Goldberg, Lisa Robinson and other *heavyweights,* gossiping about goings-on in *the music business,* I didn't shy away. But when Danny Fields introduced us, the only thing I clearly remember saying to him was that I too was from Long Island. "Oh Really?" was his dead-pan response.

Actually, getting to know Lou Reed was by a circuitous route that began before I even recorded my first note of music and was thanks to legendary music and film journalist the late Paul Nelson. A fine biography has been written about Paul[1] and you can learn quite a lot about the kind of films, music and books that Paul and I, who incorporated post WWII American pop culture into our most intimate belief system, cared so much about just by reading that book. I met Paul through a charismatic Garden City local hero, Jimmy Wilhelm, who was dating an older New York socialite and *she* was friends with the New York director of *Mercury Records*, Charlie Fasch. Jimmy, who was a fan of mine even back in my guitar hero days and had bought me my first *Marshall Amp*, through his charm and persistence, finagled his lady-friend into getting me an introduction up at *Mercury Records*. Soon after, I found myself in their offices on 57th Street, sitting in East Coast A&R Director Paul Nelson's very messy office; clogged with perilous piles of cassette demo tapes and waiting for him to take notice of me as he sat behind his desk, wearing dark glasses, a newsboy tweed cap and chain-smoking brown *Sherman Cigarillos*. When the phone rang Paul would regard it with a horrified look on his face, puff even harder on his *Sherman,* and after a half-dozen rings, reluctantly answer it. Obviously, Paul wasn't totally comfortable working in a corporate record company environment, having been quite a *personage* himself in the folk movement of the early 1960's. He was the founder of *The Little Sandy Review,* an alternative folkie magazine to the more widely read *Sing Out and* he had even had the balls to defend Bob Dylan in print when he went electric at the 1965 Newport Folk Festival while all of the other *folk Stalinists* were heaping on derision and just waiting for Bob to fail, which of course, he never did. Paul had actually gone to school with Bob Dylan at the *University of Minnesota* and had been right there at that pivotal moment in music history when Bob Dylan first heard Woody Guthrie's records and shortly thereafter *borrowed* them from Paul's unlocked room. Apparently, Paul and his roommate went looking for Bob armed with a bowling pin of all things, demanding their records back. But I was from the next generation down the line and knew nothing of this *folklore* when I showed up at his office that afternoon; I was just looking for a record deal and would have met with the devil himself to get one. In fact, in the course of my career, I did meet many devils working in the music business, but Paul Nelson was surely not one of them, in fact, he was like my guardian angel, my artistic conscience, who like me, was struggling to find his place in the treacherous skyscraper canyons of New York City.

At that first meeting, I imagine Paul was just hoping to get rid of me as painlessly as possible while placating his boss who had pressured him to take a meeting with this unknown Long Island singer-songwriter based solely on a friend of a friend's request. After numerous awkward silences, we finally got down to business and he listened to three songs from my demo cassette, and guess what, he really liked it! In fact, he loved it, even cracking a rare smile, and wanted to see me play live as soon as possible. And if that was not enough, he took me out to lunch at a fine Italian place next to Carnegie Hall where he ordered two cokes and ate *Veal Picatta*, the only things I ever saw him eat or drink in dozens of lunches together, *gratis* of his Mercury expense account. Usually, when we came into Manhattan to knock on music biz doors, Geraldine and I fed ourselves by borrowing her parents *Lord and Taylor*[2] credit card and eating dainty watercress sandwiches at the department store's *Birdcage Café*[3] surrounded by blue-haired matrons who stared at my snakeskin boots in envy or horror, not sure which, so to eat a real lunch in a 7th Avenue show business hangout was already a good sign that I was getting somewhere.

Paul Nelson, through some deal with the *Velvet Underground's* ex-manager, had scheduled to release *Live 1969*, the band's posthumous live album on *Mercury Records* and once knowing my adoration for the Velvet's *Loaded* album, he asked me, a complete unknown, to write liner notes for *Live 1969*. I took the acetates[4] of the album back to Garden City and started putting my impressions on a yellow legal pad as the songs streamed by on my record player. This was months before I even began recording my own first album and still, to this day, fans bring me that gate-fold VU album, whose liner notes begin with my words, *"Its one hundred years from today and everyone who is reading this is dead ..."* to sign as if it was one of my own records. I'm honored that my name is there on a historic album with songs by one of my favorite and most inspirational songwriters, plus it's my first appearance on any album at all, but more importantly those liner notes contained hints of the suburban fear and loathing that would become even more apparent when *Aquashow* came out. In my notes, I wrote about the thoughts that must pass through a parent's mind when they find their teenage daughter listening to the Velvet Underground's song *Heroin* and my hopes that this music would be taught in school at some point in the future, a distant hundred years from then. And guess what? The music of the *Velvet Underground,* as is that of and many other bands and rock artists, is *already* taught in colleges around the world and its only fifty years later! One of my own songs, *How's the Family,* was even featured in a University sociology textbook, complete with follow-up discussion topics based upon my lyrics. Don't laugh when I say that in another fifty years maybe *Born in the USA* will replace *The Star-Spangled Banner* as America's national anthem (a great idea indeed!) Also, in my liner notes, I wanted to know what Lou Reed's biggest secret was. And that, I confess, I never found out; nor am I sure if I want to.

Paul Nelson must have passed on my liner notes to Lou for his approval and apparently, Lou liked them, *really* liked them, because shortly thereafter he actually called my mother Josephine at her apartment on York Avenue[5] and had a brisk but engaging talk with her on the telephone, as I wasn't there at the time. At the end of the call my mom told him how excited I would be to hear from him and Lou asked her why. This is how she remembers it:

"*Because my son is a great admirer of yours,*" explained my mother.

"*Isn't everybody?*" Lou responded.

My next gig was booked at *The Mercer Arts Center* down in Greenwich Village, the first week of January 1973. The *MAC* was owned and run by art philanthropist Stanley Kaback whose immigrant father had made a fortune in the garment industry. Apparently,

Stanley loved fast *Lotus* sports-cars and the performing arts even if he wasn't exactly sure what he was getting into when he started booking local rock bands to play in his vast theatrical complex. Once, he walked into the backstage bathroom as I was getting a pre-show blow-job (what's wrong with that?) and wasn't amused even when I tried my best to legitimize an *awkward* situation by explaining I was playing there that night and the lady in question was my fiancé, just trying to calm my pre-show jitters. The beehive complex of theatres, cabarets and restaurant that made up *The Mercer Arts Center* was part of a larger structure that was attached to a sprawling welfare hotel, *The Broadway Central*, and, wouldn't you know it, a few years later the whole damn thing collapsed in a pile of rubble. But in the early 1970's, The *MAC* courageously presented nightly shows of mostly unknown acts including Patti Smith, *KISS*, and most importantly *The New York Dolls*, who with their outrageousness in style and dress were taking New York by storm, high-heels, mascara and all. *The Mercer* was also the first theater to stage Ken Kesey's *One Flew Over the Cuckoo's Nest,* long before the Milos Forman[6] film adaptation starring Jack Nicholson came out a few years after.

Paul Nelson came down to my show as promised, with fellow *Mercury* A&R man and journalist Bud Scoppa tagging along. I was billed as *Elliott Murphy's Aquashow* and me and my Garden City born and bred band, which included brother Matthew dressed in white satin pants on bass, whipped through all my original songs plus a steamy encore of *Martha and The Vandellas* hit, *Heat Wave*. You wouldn't have known it by the way he sat motionless throughout the whole set, but Paul was blown away by the show, even recording it on a cassette which I have to this day. Bud Scoppa was also wildly enthusiastic, *bopping* along to my music much more then Paul was capable of, and after the show Bud told me he was in the midst of writing an article for *Penthouse* about the *New York Dolls* and the burgeoning downtown *glam rock* scene that he would like to include me in. I wasn't sure if I was really *glam*[7] but I was prominently featured in the next month's edition of *Penthouse* along with a photo of *New York Dolls* singer David Johansen who later became a very amusing drinking buddy and friend when we were downtown neighbors. Bud's piece was possibly the first article about the New York *glam* rock scene written for a national magazine and I must have bought a dozen copies of *Penthouse* at my local newsstand to spread around. "Guess you know the girl inside," snickered the seller in the newspaper kiosque. *"I'm* inside," I replied. He couldn't figure that one out.

As nobody in the music business was going to schlep out to Long Island to see us play, Matthew and I were booking shows at *Kenny's Castaways* and other showcase venues, literally any place that would have us; I even did a solo spot at the *Improv* in *Hell's Kitchen* where comedians Richard Pryor and Robert Klein started their careers. During the day, we'd be back on Broadway, *knock, knock, knocking* on every record company door we could locate in Manhattan's yellow pages. *Warner Brothers* A&R person Mary Martin was the most encouraging, wanting to hear more songs, and promising to send a copy of our demo to their west coast office who would listen to it ... sometime. I soon figured out that if you wanted to get your demo listened to by the right people any time soon, and not thrown on a towering pile that could resemble the final scene in *Raiders of the Lost Ark*[8], having a high-powered music business connection on your side was essential. Now here's a tale of improbable synchronicity and parallel universes for the rock history books: my cousin Joan Arthurs had been married for a brief while to Wes Farrell, the co-writer of *Boys* (which the Beatles covered), *Hang on Sloopy* (which was a smash for The McCoy's, sung by Rick Derringer with whom I once auditioned for a guitar player gig in his band), and most profitably, the musical producer of the long-running TV sitcom *The Partridge Family*[9]. The last time I had seen Wes was at his and my cousin's wedding, which took place in 1966, about a year after my father's death. All I remember of that night is that *Jay and The Americans* were the house band and that as there was an open bar and being seventeen, I got as drunk as I could. By the time I was looking for a record deal in 1973, Wes had both power and prestige in the music business with an enviable track record of success. I tried on numerous occasions to reach out to him, ask his help, advice, whatever, and finally managed to set up an appointment at his mid-town office. As my brother and I remember it, Wes came out to the reception area where we were waiting to say a warm but very brief hello before quickly passing us on to an underling whose name I forget. Wes and my cousin Joan were divorced by then and he had just married Frank Sinatra's younger daughter Tina, so I was not really *family* anymore and that's as far as it went. But what's uncanny is that about at this same time, Bruce Springsteen was *also* trying to contact Wes Farrell and was *also* passed on to an underling named Mike Appel who shortly thereafter quit The Wes Farrell Organization and became Bruce's manager, eventually getting Bruce his now historic audition before the legendary A&R man, John Hammond, who had signed Bob Dylan and Billie Holiday, which led to his Columbia Records recording contract.

Today, wary of plagiarism lawsuits, all the major record labels refuse to even open an envelope containing an *unsolicited demo*, and the story of how my eventual record contract with Polydor Records unfolded could never happen in today's security obsessed world. My brother Matthew came up with the idea of visiting *Polydor*, the new kid in town, at their Broadway offices. We knew literally nothing about Polydor, only that both James Brown and the late guitar wizard Roy Buchanan had found a home there, and that it was co-owned by German and Dutch conglomerates. Everyone seemed to say that most of the *Polydor USA* start-up money had gone to James Brown who was given free reign at the label plus his own *imprint label* plus a suite of offices for when he came to town *plus* the firm stipulation in his contract that he was to be addressed as *Mr. Brown*. Get down!

When Matthew and I emerged from the elevator at 1775 Broadway and walked into the empty Polydor reception area, we really didn't know what would happen or what we should do or say, but at least we knew we looked good, both of us sporting our best

European bought wardrobe, and shoulder length blond hair. The receptionist, a pretty young black girl, friendlier then most and probably new on the job, asked *what we wanted*, rather than who we were there to see and innocently enough, we just blurted out that we wanted someone in the A&R department to listen to our demo.

"*Like now?*" she asked.

We looked at each other. "*Well yeah ... like now,*" said Matthew with his best Jack Nicholson smile.

The receptionist picked up the phone while motioning us to take a seat, which we did, both of us picking up copies of *Billboard* magazine, trying to look professional. Within minutes, out walked Shelly Snow, a young and attractive staffer from the Polydor A&R department, who shook our hands and brought us back to her little office where there was a *Revox* tape machine. Luckily, we had brought the original *reel-to-reel* tape with us and she nimbly threaded our tape to the machine and listened through the whole thing while we sat there not knowing what to do. Are you supposed to dance to your own music at moments like these or stay cool? I remember focusing on Shelly's diaphanous white silk blouse. After it was finished, and the tape end was slapping on the reel, we were shocked when she spoke right up saying, number one, *its good*, and number two, would we be able to come to *Bill's Instrument Rentals* for an audition with Peter K. Siegel, the head of A&R, later in the week. We said, *yes ma'am!* and walked out of that office two feet off the ground. Only later did I realize how attuned Shelly must have been to Peter's taste in music and everything else as they were married at the time. Two brothers meet a husband and wife team. *How's the family*, indeed!

Back in Garden City, we excitedly told the other band members the news and rehearsed for the big day. The rehearsal hall would supply the list of gear we'd need for the audition: amps, drums and keyboards, so all we had to do was look good, grab our guitars and drive into the city. Peter Siegel was tall, liked to dress in fine pinstriped suits, had Dylan-like curly hair and was maybe six years older than me. He was (and still is) an excellent banjo player and a veteran of the Greenwich Village folk scene of the early 1960's, where his group, *The Even Dozen Jug Band*, featured future hit making singer Maria Muldair (*Midnight at The Oasis*) and guitarist Steve Katz (who went on to form *The Blues Project, Blood Sweat and Tears* and would produce my third album *Night Lights*.) More synchronicity: *The Even Dozen Jug Band's* album for Elektra Records was produced by Paul Rothschild who produced my second album *Lost Generation* for RCA and most of the *Doors* albums as well. Now I live in Paris where Jim Morrison is buried at *Pere La Chaise* cemetery and, if you believe Dee Pak Chopra, coincidences are not to be dismissed. I'll go with that ...

On that fateful spring afternoon in 1973, we all knew that Peter Siegel was the *decider,* so when he walked into that no-nonsense rehearsal room and he and Shelly Snow pulled up two rickety chairs, sat down and told us to start playing whenever we were ready, I was as nervous as I'd ever been. We played a half dozen of my original songs with no big *train wrecks*, so I guess I succeeded in demonstrating to Peter that I could both sing and play guitar with enough confidence for him to take the next step. I had rehearsed the band well in the basement of my mother's last Garden City house, that dreaded refuge on Bayberry Avenue, and each band member bought a large dressing mirror at the *Salvation Army* store and placed it so that they could see themselves while performing. I wanted all of us to get our stage moves *down*. At the end of our last number, very nonchalantly, Peter stood up and pulled me aside, told me I had a deal waiting at *Polydor Records* and advised me to get a lawyer. *So that's how it happens*, I thought at the time, *simple as that, so straightforward*... until...

Even before the recording contract was fully negotiated, Peter Siegel was reaching out to producers and was recording more demos with us at *Electric Lady Studios*. I had an uneasy feeling that something unforeseen was looming on the horizon because whenever *Polydor* called, it seemed that only Matthew and I, and not the other band members, were asked to come into the city for meetings and demo sessions. We soon got the picture: the label didn't want to sign the whole band, *Elliott Murphy's Aquashow,* just the two *Murphy Brothers*. When I broke the news to the three other band members they were heartbroken, angry and extremely resentful at me for what they considered selling them out. But what could I do? My feeling was that Polydor was my last good shot at a record deal and I better take it. When I finally got the advance on future royalties of ten-thousand dollars, I gave the other three musicians in *Elliott Murphy's Aquashow* a thousand bucks each while Matthew and I split the rest one-third for him and two-thirds for me. Personally, I ended up with less than half of the total advance. Having no bank account at the time, we took the check right to Polydor's bank in Manhattan and cashed it, walking out with a short stack of one-hundred-dollar bills. For that moment, at least, I felt rich.

My rhythm guitarist, George Gates, who was Matthew's and my dearest friend, took it all more in stride then the two others – he just wanted to be in on the ride wherever that might lead. But my drummer, Greg Nickson and keyboardist Jerry Burchard never really forgave me and refused to play any more live shows after that. Jerry's wife called to tell me she hoped I would have a heart attack and die like my father before angrily hanging up. My always pragmatic brother Matthew, who went on to be a tour manager to the stars (*Talking Heads, The Eurythmics,* Brian Ferry, Steve Martin) got past this *bump in the road* quickly and immediately sized up the situation for what it was, *Elliott, they want to sign us and that's great!* But I, as is my wont, was haunted by guilt and indecision. Decades later, when I told this story to my friend Bruce Springsteen, his take on it was simple: that it was up to the label who they wanted to sign, not me. Bruce is (as one of his songs attests) *Tougher than the Rest* but I was not - I was easily influenced, over-trusting, highly sensitive, and about to enter perhaps the worst business in the world for that personality type. Trust me, I've gotten a lot tougher over the years.

Because of the inability of The New York Dolls to fit in to American radio playlists, or maybe just because of his *own* inability to fit in to a major label A&R position, Paul Nelson did eventually lose his job at *Mercury* Records. But he continued writing about the music, books and films he cared passionately about, not only reviewing my next two albums for *Rolling Stone*, where he had become the chief review editor, but also being instrumental in supporting the career of *gonzo* singer-songwriter Warren Zevon, who broke though with his 1978 *Werewolves of London* single, somewhat vindicating Paul, not to mention that he did try to sign Bruce Springsteen to Mercury as well. For me, Paul could have been as much of an *avatar* as the legendary John Hammond, if the times were different. Then, or so I heard, there was a dispute at *Rolling Stone* over introducing the *star system* - one to five - in album reviews and Paul resigned in protest which, although maybe a courageous move packed with integrity, was bucking a tide that continues to this day. After *Rolling Stone,* Paul disappeared off the radar and we lost touch. I heard he was working in a video store down in Greenwich Village and then as a copy editor for *The Jewish Weekly*. Then, after his tragic death in 2006, of what some even attributed to starvation, and I attribute to total neglect from the music business, his son Mark found his early *Mercury Records* memos while cleaning out the files in his cramped apartment. Mercury had offered me a five-thousand-dollar advance to sign with them and even in terms of new artists' deals, which are notoriously low-ball and one-sided in every legal sense possible, the Mercury offer was crap. *Polydor Records* had offered me double, ten thousand dollars, and Paul, desperate to sign me, was trying to get *Mercury* to equal that. Mark discovered a memo from Paul to his *Mercury* bosses saying that if they matched the Polydor offer they could take the extra $5000 out of his own pay if I didn't recoup in record sales. I guarantee you that such a gesture by an A&R executive, risking his own income to sign a totally unknown artist, was unheard of then or now. And Paul never told me about it.

The last time I saw Paul Nelson was in the mid 1980's; I was playing a weekly gig at *Tramps* on 15th Street, where there were rarely more than fifty or sixty people in the club. I was on stage when he walked in alone, sitting down at a table, lighting up a *Shermans* cigarette, same tweed cap, same dark glasses. We talked after the show and it was kind of stilted and awkward, neither one of us being able to *own* up to our reduced circumstances. Finally, as I walked Paul out of the noisy club, we stood alone together in front of the entrance where my name was written on a small sign in the window, *Appearing tonight ...* I asked Paul if he had seen any of Bruce Springsteen's *Born in the USA Tour*, which was breaking attendance records all across the country. I remember he shook his head and looked at me with a world-weary gaze, finally saying, *You know Elliott, it could have gone either way.* I'm not sure if it really could have but for me, that was vindication enough.

ENTERING INTO THE MUSIC BUSINESS, YOUNG, INNOCENT AND desperate to *make it* and *party*, is akin to being dropped into a pool of sharks and told to start swimming very fast record-breaking laps under disco lights. Fairly quickly, to your ever-increasing paranoia, you realize that with rare exception *they* will take almost everything you have to give if you don't put up some kind of fight. Managers wanted 50% of my song publishing and intended to keep it long after we had ceased working together; record labels were ready to withhold 10% from record royalties for *breakage,* a throwback to the nineteen-forties and the then fragile 78 rpm records; booking agents take a 15% commission off the gross income, while knowing full well that most of what you walk out the door with after a live show will be eaten up by expenses such as sound, lights, travel and crew. When I started to ask awkward questions to record companies, managers, publishers and agents, I was often stonewalled with a phrase I came to detest: *these are the standards of the industry.* Which is pretty funny for an industry that regrettably has so few standards. Read any rock biography and the evidence backs me up; young bands and artists usually get shafted one way or another, from the *Rolling Stones* down to all the unknowns, it's almost inevitable. So, you get your own *hired gun*, a music business attorney, to defend your rights, to cover your back when contracts half an inch thick arrive in your mail and you're out on tour. Then the legal bills start mounting, and you're just hoping against hope, that whatever moderate success you might achieve will cover the ever-deepening hole you're falling into financially. In fairness, I can't say if any other business is fairer or more just because the music business is all I know, and, like family, I suppose I still love it in spite of its shortcomings.

In 1983 I had dinner with the late Claude Nobs at his mountain chalet in Switzerland with two members of the iconic UK band *Queen*. Claude was the founder and the *force majeure* behind the *Montreux Jazz Festival* and after booking me to play that year's festival, he had graciously invited me to check out his *postcard perfect* chalet overlooking Lac Leman. In between courses of *raclette* and *fondue*, I asked Roger Taylor, the drummer and co-songwriter of *Queen*, how does an artist ever really make any money in the music business? It just seems impossible! Roger said it was actually quite simple - you've just got to have two huge hit albums, one following right after the other.

"Why two?" I asked.

"With the money you make from the first hit album you hire all the lawyers and accountants you'll need to free you from all the bad contracts you were obliged to enter into to even have that hit in the first place," Roger replied.

"But where does that leave you?" I asked.

"Moneywise? Probably close to zero," he laughed, *"but free to record that next album, which if it makes it might set you up for life."*

Kind of like the second mouse getting the cheese, I thought. I remember wise Claude Nobs quickly adding, *"A little talent never hurts either."*

Once the *Polydor* deal was signed, Matthew and I, with faithful friend George tagging along, headed west to Los Angeles to begin recording with Thomas Jefferson Kaye, who seemed at the time like a good choice for producer due to his recent hit *Dead Skunk in the Middle of the Road* by another new Dylan (although no one was calling me that yet), Louden Wainwright III. *Polydor* got us rooms at the Westwood *Holiday Inn* and a rental car from *Hertz* and when I caught a glimpse of the Amazonian blonds who in the early 70's drove the *Hertz* shuttle bus at LAX airport were wearing canary yellow hot-pants, surely totally politically incorrect today, I didn't know if I was in paradise or on the set of *Shindig*[10]. It was my first time in LA and I soaked it in: the palm trees, the surfing beaches, the fresh OJ at *Duke's Coffee Shop*[11], eating dinner at *The Brown Derby* on Wilshire Boulevard, my booth straddled between those of actor George Kennedy, who co-starred in *Cool Hand Luke*, and big-band era trumpet player Harry James, who was married to WWII pin-up queen Betty Grable. It was like being transported back in time to a Hollywood from another era. But in spite of all that cool west coast *karma*, the recording sessions were a disaster. Thomas Jefferson Kaye was living on *Kahlua and Crème* and, I think, a lot of *nose candy*, and almost immediately any bonding we had done in New York began to become unglued as we didn't see eye to eye creatively or any other way. Tommy was set on *dumbing down* my sound to that of a completely manufactured country rock singer and when he slowed down my best song, *Last of the Rock Stars,* on our first day of recording at *Village Recorders*, I put my foot (and guitar) down and retreated back to the *Holiday Inn*, trying to get up the courage to call New York and tell *Polydor*, sorry guys, this isn't working as we all thought it would. The night after the aborted session, Matthew, George and I went to the *Rainbow Bar and Grill* on Sunset Boulevard, to drown our sorrows and figure out our next move. What if *Polydor* insisted I stay in LA and finish the album with Tommy or, even worse, what if they dropped the project altogether and we found ourselves back in Garden City rehearsing in the basement, our three glum faces reflecting back to us in the mirrors in our rehearsal space? Still, in spite of all those risks, I was adamant; I had definite sounds and arrangements already in my head for these songs and as much as

I love and respect country music, that was not to be me. While sitting at the *Rainbow*, I reached back to stretch my arms out wide and in doing so, I bumped against somebody's shoulder. Turning around to apologize, I was knocked silent by the vision before me. It was like I had stumbled upon the setting for a Da Vinci like *Last Supper on Sunset Strip* because sitting at that table was Jack Nicholson, Joni Mitchell and, if that wasn't enough, the person who I had bumped into was none other than Bob Dylan himself. I grunted out some kind of apology and soon after Bob left this star-studded group and got into a light blue station wagon and quickly drove off. We quickly got up from our table and followed him as best we could, but he lost us among the palm trees of *Beverly Hills*. If ever in my life I had a clear *sign* of what to do that was it ...

That literal *brush* with greatness gave me enough confidence, that after one farewell *Kahlua and Crème* with Tommy Kaye, it was *hasta luego baby* and we high-tailed it back to New York to, hopefully, start all over again. I even gave Polydor back what was left of my *per diem* money, something their accountant said had never happened before in all his years working for a record company and something I would never do again. Peter K. Siegel, to his credit and to my everlasting gratitude, was both sympathetic to my plight and to show he still believed in the project, agreed to produce the album himself at New York's *Record Plant* Studio B on West 44th Street. With a few phone calls and plane tickets, Peter quickly assembled an amazing backing band, including *bro* Matthew on bass, *Byrds* alumni Gene Parsons on drums, *Highway 61* keyboard player Frank Owens on organ and many other top session players of the day. During office hours, Peter was obliged to fulfill his A&R duties at *Polydor,* so while he sat behind his desk, the band rehearsed at *Bills Instrument Rentals* and I was able to teach these fine musicians the arrangements to my songs as I believed they should be played and with a classic rock sound – plenty of jangly *Fender* guitar, rich *Hammond* organ and cool *Rhodes* electric piano - that would stand the test of time. The actual sessions began around seven PM and some nights I would get so stressed, so anxious, that Matthew and I would retreat to the studio building's rooftop and gaze out onto the seemingly infinite lights of Manhattan's skyline, trying to de-stress. Still in my Hepatitis recovery stage, I was not drinking or even smoking pot and learning to deal with my emotions raw and unfiltered, reacting to every musical moment we passed in that studio like my life depended on it, which, in a way, it did.

Other rock musicians apparently didn't find putting their music down on magnetic recording tape nearly as stressful as I did, because conversely, just down the elevator, on the ground floor in *Record Plant Studio A,* camped (and I do mean *camped*) *The New York Dolls,* who Paul Nelson had signed to *Mercury* Records, putting the finishing touches on their eponymous first album with wizard producer Todd Rundgren. When I went down to visit, I had the impression that the *Sunset Strip Riots* had moved to the west side of Manhattan because man, was there a party going on! Band members, girlfriends, groupies, crew and hanger-ons were everywhere, all drinking, smoking, partying and looking *uber-Glam.* The notable exception, of course, was Paul Nelson, still wearing his newsboy cap, smoking *Shermans* and nearly hidden out of view in the corner of the control room; knowing full well that his job depended on the success of this album. In stark contrast, my own sessions, ten stories above in *Studio B,* were almost solemn affairs, with just Peter K. Siegel and engineer Shelly Yakus (who was nominated into the Rock and Roll Hall of Fame in 1999) sitting behind the control board while us five musicians concentrated on the song charts in front of us. No party to be found, but still, I believe, everyone who was there having a sense that something memorable was going down on tape.

When it came time to shoot the cover for *Aquashow,* I was looking for an album cover version of *cinema vérité,* something real, already deciding that all my album covers henceforth would be shot in hotels, something I've done ... only twice. For me, the obvious hotel location to begin with would be the *Palm Court* of the *Plaza Hotel,* where Jay Gatsby courted Daisy. The label went along with my vision and hired a wonderful photographer, Jack Mitchell, who had been shooting Broadway and ballet stars, for the session. I had one favor to ask him: could he reproduce the blurry effect on the Rolling Stones album *Between the Buttons* where there seemed to be a circle of distortion around the frame. He achieved that effect easily enough, but in hindsight maybe that was a mistake because the same effect had been used on Dylan's *Bringing it all Back Home* album cover and it made the comparison too easy. Placed on the back of the album was a vintage photograph of my father's show, *Elliott Murphy's Aquashow*, with a line of bathing beauties all holding red and white domed umbrellas. Art designer Paula Bisacca found a similar umbrella at *Uncle Sam's Umbrella* in Manhattan and while I posed in front of an art-deco urn, brother Matthew sat behind me holding that umbrella above him. How could I know that ten years later I would be working in that *same* umbrella company, as a *temp secretary*, broke, newly sober, nearly forgotten by the music business and so ashamed of my fall from grace that when acclaimed Rolling Stone photographer Annie Liebowitz came in one day to pick up an umbrella for another photo shoot, I hid under the desk.

To promote *Aquashow,* I was sent out on tour with my band primarily opening for *The Kinks*. I had been a fan of Ray Davies from the very first time I heard *You Really Got Me* which, for my son, is a *Van Halen* song! Opening for the *Kinks* almost felt like I was opening for *The Beatles* or *The Stones* as they too were bonified members of the *British invasion*, that mid-sixties generation who taught us how to look and act like rock genuine rock musicians, playing in a band, in ways that Elvis, an almost other-worldly iconoclast that we could hardly imitate, never could. My publicist at the time, Laura Kaufmann, was a close friend of Ray's and anxious to get us together. She knew how unhappy I was with *Polydor* and also that Ray was starting up his own label, *Konk Records,* figuring perhaps there was a match to be made that could really work creatively for everybody. True enough, as Ray and I were both *wordy* songwriters who drew from a sometimes-similar palette of ideas and inspirations – Ray had *Cellu-*

loid Heroes and I had *Marilyn*, Ray had *Well Respected Man* and I had *White Middle Class Blues*. The Kinks tour got underway with no snags; it was indeed a good match, and the *Kinks* audience loved us. The tour included a memorable concert at *Hofstra College*, just a few miles from where I was brought up, where *Newsweek* writer Maureen Orth came to cover the show and profiled me in the magazine, along with Billy Joel, in an article about a new genre of pop music: *suburban rock*. Ray and I hadn't had time for much more than a brief *hey man!* during soundchecks until finally a day off came when both bands were stranded in Richmond, Virginia, all of us chilling in the same hotel, which just so happened to overlook the Virginia State Penitentiary. That evening, Laura brought Ray Davies up to my hotel room and we talked music and future plans, but all the time I noticed Ray never took off his overcoat and had an obvious air of distraction about him; thinking to myself he was just a reserved English gentleman. But when we both found ourselves staring out the window to the grim looking prison just next store, whose high walls were doused with bright klieg lights, the conversation stalled. Suddenly Ray pointed to the prison and said that the guy at the hotel front desk had told him that when there's an execution and a prisoner gets strapped into the electric chair, the prison lights actually dim for a moment as the current is drained from the grid and directed to some poor soul's shaved head. And just then, as we were both standing there, peering out the window, I swear the prison lights dimmed. Ray looked at me in horror, quickly excused himself, and I never signed with *Konk Records*. Even a marvelous songwriter such as him, I suppose, can be superstitious.

    All this time, Matthew and I were trying to find the right manager who could take the tremendous buzz surrounding *Aquashow* and transform it into a real career. Our lawyer, a fellow Long Islander, Gerald Margolis gave us a perspective list to check out and, let me tell you, it was slim pickings. Among the most promising was a new venture called *Management 3* which consisted of partners Sid Bernstein (who had promoted the *Beatles* at Shea Stadium), Billy

Fields (who worked with Neil Diamond) and the legendary Jerry Weintraub who promoted both Elvis and Dylan and dominated the meeting. I must say that these pros were gracious and treated us as equals although in reality we were nothing but rookies groping our way in the dark. As we were about to leave, I remember Jerry Weintraub gesturing for us to follow him to his office, opening his closet, and showing us a few of his many outfits hanging there, "This is what I wear when I'm with Elvis," he said pulling out a flamboyant denim jacket decorated with chrome studs, like something a member of the *Memphis Mafia* might sport on a Saturday night out, "And this is what I wear when I'm with Frank Sinatra," pointing to a classy dark suit. He went on to show us a few more examples of his sartorial matches for various well-known acts he handled. It was like the scene in *The Great Gatsby* where Gatsby proudly shows off to Daisy all his hand-made shirts. "You see, I'm flexible," Jerry explained. "I can adapt to any artist I work with." And, as his history has shown, he certainly could. After *Rocky Mountain High* success as John Denver's manager, he became a formidable film producer, a true *Hollywood Tycoon,* producing Robert Altman's *Nashville* as well as the George Clooney, Brad Pitt remake of *Oceans 11*. I only met Jerry Weintraub that one brief time, but he was so unforgettable, that I always followed his career from afar. In 2015 he passed away and strangely enough, I'll miss him if only as a memorable bit player in my storied past.

Chapter Five

LONG ISLAND GUYS

Elliott Murphy & Lou Reed 1975

*S*oon after *Aquashow*'s release, an inquiring journalist for the *New York Post* had the good sense to ask Lou Reed what he thought of the album, as comparisons between myself and Lou were abound, and Lou's very positive response was reprinted and misquoted all over the place, something about the *lyrics being so real, man!* Lou and I were both Long Island guys and shared that unique accent, not so tough as our New York City neighbors (think Robert De Niro) but still with a punk edge softened by a touch of *bourgeoisie* affluence (think Alec Baldwin.) From that first call to my mother after I wrote the Velvet *Underground Live 1969* liner notes, Lou and I had stayed in touch and he regularly came down to my shows at *Max's Kansas City* and later, the *Bottom Line*; he also introduced me to Andy Warhol (who once asked me if he could touch the buttons on my *Levi's 501 jeans* fly), as well as the celebrated British rock photographer Mick Rock, the same charming and talented man who shot the well-known cover for Lou's *Transformer* album, which contained *Walk on the Wild Side*. Later, after running into Mick at *The Mudd Club* on numerous late nights we decided it was time he shot one of my covers as well, and that's his photo on my first independent album, *Murph The Surf*.

Most significantly, Lou brought me to the attention of *RCA* Record, where he was then signed himself, and with the help of his manager, Dennis Katz, convinced *RCA* to pay the one-hundred-fifty-thousand-dollar *ransom* that *Polydor* was demanding to set me free. A hefty five-album deal was quickly negotiated and following the signing and the check that came with it, I bought a new red *MGB* convertible to celebrate. The plan was for Lou to produce my debut album for RCA, but you know what they say, *if you want to hear God laugh tell him your plans.*

Manager Dennis Katz, whose only clients at the time

Just A Story from America

were Lou and I, had offices on East 59th Street, a short distance away from where Lou lived in a banal sub-let apartment. The first time I visited Lou at his *home* I was shocked; first because he didn't live downtown in hipper Soho, Chelsea or the Village, as one might expect, him being the *hippest of the hip*, and second because his apartment was absolutely devoid of any personality, almost like a *Holiday Inn* room with bad motel art decorating the walls. None of this seemed to bother Lou though, who was far more interested in his new *TEAC* four-track tape machine, his multiple cassette recorders and an array of guitar effects pedals. When I first began visiting Lou in his apartment, he was living with Barbara Hodes, a vivacious fashion designer, who soon became fast friends with Geraldine and seemed to know everybody worth knowing, from artist Larry Rivers to David Bowie. Many nights we all hung out at *Ashleys* on lower 5th Avenue, a popular bar and restaurant, owned by charismatic *Alice Cooper* publicist, Ashley Pandel, where I once met John Lennon, descending the staircase with Ashley himself who was kind enough to introduce us. I was awestruck! It was John *fucking* Lennon, who once said *Before Elvis there was nothing*, and I, who could have said the same about him, was at a total loss of words, finally blurting out, *what are you doing here?* To which John replied, *I'm out getting fucked up, Elliott, what do you think I'm doing?* I followed them to Ashley's office where Mick Jagger was on the phone. Everyone seemed to be calling a drug dealer.

Barbara also took us on a bizarre visit to meet the manager of the *Who,* Chris Stamp, who lived in a very dark and spacious apartment around the corner from *Ahsley's,* in a sprawling apartment with no clocks on the wall and permanently drawn *black-out* curtains. It seemed ideal to me. I didn't know it, but I was entering my *dark* period. Chris Stamp himself later saw the light, so to speak, and worked as an addiction counselor.

But fairly soon after we met her, Barbara moved out of Lou's flat and the mysterious transvestite Rachel moved in; although in those days it was difficult to say who was a transvestite and who was just ...

fashionable. I spent a fair amount of time with Lou and Rachel, sitting around his apartment listening to the early stages of *Metal Machine Music* or riding in taxis going to downtown after hours clubs, entranced while Lou pontificated on whatever subject had him going on that particular day; telling me about the poet Delmore Schwartz who had been his professor at *Syracuse University*, and who I never heard of before Lou mentioned him. Once again, Lou was ahead of his time as Saul Bellow's Pulitzer Prize winning novel, *Humboldt's Gift*, a fictionalized version of Delmore's life and times, came out a year later in 1975. As for the shadowy Rachel, she didn't say much, keeping her thoughts to herself while putting on make-up or changing outfits, as Lou went on forever about his latest music business feud, of which he had many. He was a junkie for musical gear of all sorts and talked me into buying a used *Gibson Les Paul Jr.* guitar, I wish I had today, while trying to convince me to set out on a solo tour with just an electric guitar and leave all the critics wondering. Lou wanted nothing to do with folk music, never heard him say a good word about Bob Dylan, never saw him pick up an acoustic guitar, insisting that in the *Velvet Underground* if anyone played a blues riff, they were heavily fined.

In spite of his mercurial personality, Lou was still an undeniably motivated and gifted artist, an amazing songwriter with a voice that was perfect for ... Lou Reed songs. After the RCA deal was done he seriously began preparations to produce my album, suggesting studios and musicians, listening to the demos of my new songs where he would stop at key points, commenting with enthusiasm and insight. Perversely, Lou was very impressed by a throwaway song I had written for Geraldine, who now wanted to become a singer herself entitled, *Too Young to Be A Mother*. One evening, Lou came over to my apartment on East 80th Street, where my friend, the late Richard Sohl, who later joined The Patti Smith group, accompanied me on my *Wurlitzer* electric piano, while I sang my new songs and Lou sat nearby and took notes. We did this until the neighbors banged on the wall, and then Lou and I took a taxi down to his place and kept working until five in the morning and I could sing no more. Begging for some rest, I went back to my apartment and had been asleep for maybe two hours when my phone rang. It was Lou:

"Hey Elliott, you ready to come back so we can keep working?"

"Come on Lou, I've got to get some sleep."

"Listen man, if you're not into it ..."

I'm sure there were additional *elements* contributing to Lou's uncanny ability to stay up for days on end without any apparent sleep, other than his *strident* work ethic. The only book I ever personally saw Lou Reed read (that's funny) was the doorstop size *Physicians' Desk Reference*, an in-depth guide to prescription drugs that Lou seemed to have whole sections bookmarked. Then, unexpectedly, something happened which eventually derailed the whole project, when Lou got caught up in a drug bust out on the end of Long Island in Riverhead, I believe, involving forged prescriptions for *Desoxyn*, a pharmaceutical grade of methamphetamine. I was never privy to all the details, but I do recall walking into Dennis Katz's office one afternoon and seeing Lou sitting all alone in a vast conference room looking absolutely dreadful. I asked him where he had been?

"Jail," was all he said.

So now there was this messy legal situation that had to be dealt with, which everyone at Lou's label and management was trying to keep quiet, hoping it wouldn't interfere with the promotion of Lou's album *Sally Can't Dance*. Lou had brought me down to *Electric Lady Studios* to listen to the final mixes months before and honestly, I thought it was a fine album, great singing by Lou, and that *Ennui* was amongst his most tender and insightful ballads. At the time, Lou could not have been more positive about the album himself although in later years he seemed to have written it off completely. Not sure why. *Sally* was supposed to undo the commercial failure of the *Berlin* album that had preceded it, in much the same way as the *Rock 'n Roll Animal* live album had previously resuscitated his career. Of course, Lou followed up *Sally* with *Metal Machine Music*, an almost unlistenable collection of overlapping feedback tracks he'd recorded at home and yet, in some way I suppose, a prescient of the EDM to come. But there's a thin line between genius and madness ... wait, isn't that from *Frankenstein?*

When I say that Lou had a *mercurial* nature that is indeed an understatement and anyone who knew him back then, damn well knows what I mean. When Bruce Springsteen graciously invited Françoise and I to sit at his table at the 1992 *Rock and Roll Hall of Fame* dinner, held at the Waldorf Astoria Hotel in NYC, I spotted Lou nearby and when I went over to say hi, he barely acknowledged me. Yet just a few years later, totally unexpectedly, he called me in Paris and wanted to meet up for drinks although neither of us was drinking by then. We met in the lobby of the swanky *Hotel Plaza Athénée*, had a cafe and took a walk across the *Seine*. Always a bonafide rockstar as far as the Parisians were concerned, Lou easily got recognized, which he seemed to like, until one older Parisian lady of a *certain* age, regarding Lou in his long black overcoat with the collar up against the wind, incredulously and hysterically mistook him for a priest. She piously addressed him as *Mon Pere* and bowed her head, which Lou didn't seem to appreciate. During that walk, I gave Lou a short narration of what had happened to me in the intervening years since we were hanging out in the seventies; how I'd moved to Paris, continued to record and release albums, was constantly touring all over Europe; and, most significantly, about the birth of my son, Gaspard in 1990. Standing on the *Pont Neuf*, the oldest bridge in Paris, Lou put his hand on my shoulder and gave me that famous closed-mouth half smile of his. I remember his words to this day: *So, things worked out after all Elliott, didn't they?* He was no priest, but it felt like a benediction nonetheless.

Chapter Six

TIME TO GET FABULOUS

Sylvia Myles, Elliott Murphy & Geraldine Murphy – Russian Tea Room, NYC mid-1970s

Aquashow and the acclaim it generated both within and outside the music biz had indeed put me on the map. Soon after its release, I was at some star-studded event when Paul Simon came over to me, complimented me on my album, and wished me luck. Just a year before I had been playing his song *Mother and Child*

Reunion on the streets of Europe as passing pedestrians threw coins into my hat. What was I to think? That I had *arrived* in some fashion? Suddenly, it seemed to me that that there were no limits, no boundaries to my creative desires from this point on. I had been granted a temporary entry into the *club*, knowing that my next album had better be very special if I wanted to renew my membership. I figured what I needed was *star-power* to get me to where I wanted to go, and I started reaching out, or rather reaching up, and sent David Bowie a letter care of *RCA Records* asking him to produce my second album, telling him I wanted to make a record with the originality and class of his own breakthrough album *Hunky Dory*. I liked where Bowie was going with his songs back then, a sense of *audio-verité* with confessional lyrics and pop icons named in titles like *A Song for Bob Dylan* and *Andy Warhol*. This seemed to me to be the same territory I was trying to inhabit. After all, I considered us all to be *rock troubadours*, our job being to pass something on, *All the young dudes carry the news*[1] contagiously wrapped in infectious melodies. Like a letter in a bottle thrown into the sea, I didn't really expect to hear back from Bowie but lo and behold some months later the phone rang, and a slightly cockney accent said, *"Hi Elliott – David here - got your letter."*

    He invited me down to *Electric Lady Studio* to preview his *David Live* album at a private pre-release party. David welcomed me warmly like I was an old friend come to visit. Very bright yet soft-spoken, he told me to follow him and offered me a line of cocaine in the bathroom which I reluctantly snorted up one nostril, it being my first line of cocaine. At least, my ten-year voyage of addiction, was launched by a pedigreed *rock star* holding the spoon. When he offered me a second line I refused, not even knowing that that was the *suggested dosage*. We went back into the studio, along with about twenty-five *glam* fans, sprawled out on the carpet and listened to *David Live* from start to finish. It was utterly mind-blowing, greatest live album I had ever heard, although I'm not sure if that was the *side effects of the cocaine*[2], the *Electric Lady* sound system, or the album itself, and I should probably take another listen one of these days. I was clearly disappointed when David said he was too busy at the moment, what with his own new album and all that entailed, to produce me, and suggested instead I speak to Tony Visconti, his producer. I probably should have followed him up on that as Tony is a *genuine* producer, but I had my sights set on *star power*, even reaching out to Mick Jagger, even though he hadn't really ever shown any interest in producing other artists at all. Somehow, I managed to get word to Mick through the *Stones'* then manager Peter Rudge, who did *seem* to say that Mick was *kind of* interested in my proposal, especially since the recent formation of *Rolling Stones Records*, distributed by WEA, would allow the boys to sign and produce outside artists[3]. There were many meetings with Mick scheduled at Peter's New York office, but Mick himself never appeared. Peter said I probably would have a better chance if I had asked Keith Richards to produce my album, he was the real *studio cat* of the group, and he was probably right but a year later when I finally met Mick Jagger himself, it taught me a lesson about the price of stardom I never forgot.

Fast forward to a year later: Geraldine and I had been invited to a showcase performance by the wife of ex-*Mamas & The Papas* leader John Phillips, South African singer Geneviève Waïte, at *Reno Sweeney's,* a posh and intimate village cabaret. We both loved Genevieve's debut album, *Romance is on the rise*, as it was constantly on our turntable in my swanky new pre-war[4] apartment on East 72nd Street. It was the kind of album you liked to play while you were getting dressed to go club-hopping and calling around to drug dealers. There was something very 1920's about the mood and cover of the album and, by this time, we were taking *Scott and Zelda* dangerously too seriously as role models for our shaky marriage. But we were gaining traction as a stylish New York couple and when *Rolling Stone* did their first collection of rock stars photographs, at the suggestion of my new friend Steven Meisel, who later went on to become an acclaimed fashion photographer, Geraldine and I ducked into one of those coin-operated automated *photobooths* on *Times Square,* where they shoot four portraits in a row. Geraldine popped in for the last shot and *Rolling Stone* loved it. We were in the book *Pin-Ups* ... and we were *in*!

After Geneviève Waïte's show, those in the in-crowd were invited to a party at guitarist's Rick Derringer's house located just down the block. Rick had sung *Hang on Sloopy* with his group *The McCoys,* played guitar with albino Texas bluesman Johnny Winter, as well as doing his own solo albums, and he and his wife Liz were a scene-making inseparable couple as well. Now we're all divorced. Anyway, I walked into the party and am sitting in Rick's living room with Geraldine and our great late friend A&R executive Bob Feiden, when Mick Jagger strolls in with his then-wife, the exotic Nicaraguan beauty, Bianca. They're divorced too, by the way. After a few moments, Bianca disappears upstairs with Liz Derringer and Mick is sitting there all by his lonesome. Time goes by, the room is full of people, musicians, music biz executives, journalists and hanger-ons of all stripes, but still Mick is somewhat awkwardly sitting there alone. How could that be, I ask myself? Then I realized that everyone in that room is afraid to talk to him! And that was the big lesson: stardom attracts people when you don't want them around and leaves you lonely when you need them. Getting up a bit of courage, I stood up and faced Mick, carrying a joint with me, and hesitantly walked over to him, introducing myself, and asking him if he had received my album *Aquashow* which I had sent him the year before. *Yes,* he said. And did he like it? *Yes,* he said he did, adding, *sounded a lot like Bob Dylan,* pronouncing that name like only an Englishman can, also adding that he had just been with Bob out on the west coast. *And how's he doing?* I asked. *Very together,* said Mick, slowly repeating for emphasis. *Very ... together.* It was like when he was addressing the audience at the doomed *Altamont* festival in 1969, trying to calm things down after the Hells Angels had just stabbed concert goer Meredith Hunter. *Come on! We can get it together!*

I don't know why I said what I did next. Maybe it was because I was a Long Island wise guy, but without even thinking I blurted out, "*Do you think the old boy has got it in him to make another great album?*"

Now you have to remember, I was twenty-five, Mick was thirty-one, Bob Dylan maybe a few years older. None of us anywhere near eligible to join the AARP[5]. Mick raised his eyebrows, puckered his substantial lips, and gave me a certain look, best described as *askance*, and a long pause followed, as if he was sizing me up, almost glaring at me. "*Who is this fucking punk?*" I imagine him thinking, and this was years before the *real* punks were referring to both the *Stones* and *Beatles* and Dylan as *dinosaurs*. "*I think so,*" Mick replied slowly. "*Definitely.*"

Of course, Mick was right about Bob; *Blood on the Tracks, Desire, Time Out of Mind,* all brilliant albums, all yet to come. But at that time, in the mid-70's, we were still dealing with the radical change of style of *Self-Portrait* and *Nashville Skyline* and we didn't yet know that we would grow to love those Bob Dylan albums as well as the years opened our ears and time sprinkled the magic dust of history over everything Bob Dylan ever touched while he set out on his appropriately named, *Never Ending Tour*. There will come a day when *George Washington slept here* will be replaced by *Bob Dylan sang here*.

I reached into my pocket and offered Mick the joint I was holding, and we passed it between us. Each time I put it to my mouth he encouraged me to smoke more, take deeper drags, and I did. Thanks for that Mick! Then Bianca came downstairs and whisked him away. Years later, when Keith Richards released his solo album *Talk is Cheap* and I was sometimes working as a journalist for *Rolling Stone, Spin,* and a number of European music magazines, I interviewed Keith for the leading Italian Rock magazine of the day, *Mucchio Selvaggio*.

The appointment with Mr. Richards was set for Monday at noon sharp. At 11 a.m. I get a call – "*Keith can't make it – dentist appoint-*

ment – let's moved it 'till Tuesday." Then another call Tuesday morning to say, "*Keith is stuck.*"

"*What do you mean stuck?*" I asked – they didn't know, *just stuck.* The interview is moved to Wednesday ... and this went on all week until my Friday deadline was looming. OK the interview will definitely take place Friday at noon – then a call – Oh no! I thought – "*No worries,*" they said, "*Keith is definitely coming, just make it 2 p.m.*"

"*Why,*" I asked. Because he's *stuck ... again.* So, I get to Keith's management office at two and Keith strolls in just before three, gives me a quick nod and a wave before disappearing into an inner office, coming out twenty minutes later with a bottle of *Rebel Yell Bourbon* gripped in his *skull ring* hand and a broad smile on his face, announcing that, "*Dr. Richards will see you now,*" punctuated by his unmistakable, should be *patented*, devilish chuckle. His well-practiced charm oozed over me like a slow blues number and all was forgiven, of course. Keith took a seat across from me while I stared at his skull ring, wondering if I should kiss it. "*So, they tell me you're a musician,*" he said by way of opening. "*What do you play?*" I wasn't surprised that he hadn't heard of me. I doubt if he had listened to much music recorded after 1956.

I play ... guitar, I said, feeling about twelve years old, like I had just walked out of *Manny's Music Store* with my new *Kent* electric guitar in hand.

"*That damn thing!*" said Keith.

And if you don't believe me go on my website and you can hear it yourself in *his master's voice.*

Unbeknownst to me at the time, there was to be a happy ending to *Aquashow*, at least for me personally, a kind of saving grace, but that wouldn't come about until some forty years later when I re-recorded all ten tracks from that album, re-titled it *Aquashow Decon-*

structed, and it thus it landed safely into the 21st Century. A worthy effort, well worth the time and cost involved, said many critics who were familiar with the original, and I thank them for that, but what made this re-visitation much more significant and meaningful, at least to me, is that it was produced and arranged by my son Gaspard Murphy, then twenty-four years old, the same age I was when I made the original back in 1973. The strings are re-strung as the torch is passed. The songs themselves withstood the test of time and the reviews were very satisfying (French *Rolling Stone* gave it four stars). Listen carefully and you can hear my voice choking up when I sing the last verse of *How's the Family* one more time after forty years or more gone by, sitting in the vocal booth of Paris studio *Question de Son* with my son listening on the other side of the glass partition and me singing from the other side of time.

How's the boy and the girl and the lives that lie ahead
And from two they join as one - they say we'll love till we are dead...

I only now appreciate how much my first album was an homage to my departed father, a way of reconnecting with him, of calling out through time and space, *we are alive!* I had an eerie feeling, even back then, that this intensely personal first album, no matter how highly it might have been praised by the critics and in spite of the significant radio play *Last of the Rock Stars* was getting, that it was doomed to fail commercially, at least at first. My friend Kenny Meisalas, a one-time punk musician who is now a top deal-maker for recording artists such as P. Diddy and Lady Gaga, says the music business is a business that breaks hearts and believe me when I say, he wasn't talking about the hearts of the public.

The amount of work, sacrifice and heartache that can go into writing and recording an album, making sure every melody weaves its way to the next without the seams showing, that every chorus is monumental, that every verse tells a story, that every *bridge* tells the same story in a different way, that every musician plays his instrument in impeccable and inspired fashion, that the engineer manages to catch the best take and record it onto tape or hard-drive without distortion or drop-outs, that the mix puts all those parts back together in a way that will catch the ear of even the most casual listener, and finally, that the album cover succeeds in visually conveying that indefinable concept of an artist's identity, along with the vision of the music he's offering, in an appealing package that will seduce the public ... and so much more, is mind boggling. And then the *thing* actually comes out, *released* is what they use to call it although hip hop artists like to now say *drop a record* which is way cooler. Whatever you want to call it, at that moment the album is officially born, a day circled in your mind's calendar perhaps a year in advance, and within a few months everything you've put your heart and soul into gets praised or damned by critics or, as in the summation of artist/critic relations expert Lou Reed, *Could you imagine working for a year and you get a B+ from some asshole in the Village Voice?* And even more important, is to be blessed by the all-powerful forces of radio who decide to put one or two tracks into *heavy rotation*. In most cases, after the dust settles, you just hope you sold enough so that the label will give you the green light to move on to the next album. That's where you heart starts breaking. When you have to leave the last album behind and move on to the next ...

Chapter Seven

LOST GENERATION IN LA LA LAND

Elliott Murphy record store promo 1975

My second album *Lost Generation* was supposed to be the one that would deliver the payoff that *Aquashow* was denied due to *Polydor's* poor handling of it. I was now on *RCA Records*, a respected major label, a definite step up from *Polydor*, maybe not as classy as *Columbia* or as hip as *Atlantic* or with the laid-back west coast vibe of *Warner Bros*, but still, *RCA* was home to Elvis Presley, *The Kinks*, *Jefferson Airplane*, David Bowie and Lou Reed himself and that was *bono fides* enough for me. Thanks to my new manager Dennis Katz, I had a really generous and long-term contract, the kind of deal that new artists are rarely offered today. *Artist development* was a valid concept back in the day, when labels understood that it was extremely rare for any artist or band to break on their first album, so new acts were given years and multiple albums to develop their talents, get their *mojo* working, before being expected to reap profits from the masses. But things have changed and today, you need a huge million hits on *YouTube* before you can get a record company's attention. But as Lou Reed sang in *Sweet Jane*[1], and I remind myself every day, *Those were different times ...*

Although my signing to RCA Records received much attention in the music trade mags *Billboard, Cash Box* and *Record World,* it was a bittersweet triumph for me personally because the truth was that I always wanted to work with the music biz's star executive, Clive Davis, who had come to one of my shows at *Max's Kansas City* and had now begun his own label *Arista Records*. My friend, A&R executive Bob Feiden, had followed Clive to *Arista* and was personally trying to shepherd a deal for me there. Dennis Katz, on the other hand, was pushing me towards *RCA* because, although Clive's enthusiasm was substantial his offer, understandably, was not, as *Arista* was a new label with limited resources. There I was, Lou Reed and Dennis Katz pushing me towards *RCA*[2] on the one hand and Clive Davis welcoming me to be among his first signings at *Arista* on the other. What did I do? Well ... I took the money and ran to *RCA*, a decision I have often regretted but what the hell. There is the famous story of George Bernard Shaw coming to Hollywood following an offer to write scripts for Hollywood tycoon Sam Goldwyn wherein Shaw defined the difference between an artist and a businessman: "*Do you know, Mr. Goldwyn, there is a radical difference between you and me? You are only interested in art and I am only interested in money.*" That doesn't say it all, but it says a lot.

Being signed to RCA provided me with a sense of financial security that I had not felt since the death of my father. I had money in the bank while I figured out, how to follow-up *Aquashow*. I knew the critics would both be cheering me on and, at the same time, gunning for me. And all of this, to say the least, was making me anxious. My response to the stress? Go shopping for a new apartment, buy myself a red *MGB* convertible, and, in a very bad series of decisions, develop a serious cocaine addiction. It's written somewhere that *we will not regret the past* and even with all of those bad life-style choices, I managed to write many of the songs which have stood the test of time right up until this day. I also was bored with the *bard of* suburbia title and was desperate to get past it, to move on to a bigger canvas. In my next album, I wanted to let the fertile fields of suburban angst fade far, far away in my rear-view mirror and took on a plethora of unsolvable worldly evils as my source material: the criminal justice system, prostitution and the plight of Vietnam veterans (one in each verse of *Lost Generation*) the troubling appearance of fashionable neo-Nazism (*Eva Braun*) and even the music business itself (*Manhattan Rock*). Hadn't there been enough mindless love songs already? Wasn't pop culture ready to move on to deeper waters? Apparently not.

IN 1974, SOON AFTER GETTING OFF THE ROAD WITH THE KINKS and *Jefferson Starship*, my brother Matthew, with friend and guitarist George Gates behind the wheel, got into a shattering car wreck, both physically and emotionally, on Long Island's *Northern State Parkway*, flipping over George's *Porsche 911* on the very first day he bought it. Geraldine and I got the news from my mother after returning from a late night at Lou Reed's apartment and rushed out to *North Shore Hospital* where Matt and George had been taken by ambulance. They were both in frightening shape, and as I approached the emergency ward I could hear their moaning. The most serious of Matthew's injuries had been breaking both his shoulder blades – his *scapula* - when he was thrown from the car. Poor George had fractured his *femur* (thigh bone), apparently the largest bone in the body, and would have to undergo a series of operations, one of which almost proved fatal when the anesthesia travelled to his lungs. That accident and its aftermath would shape both of their futures in immutable ways. Coming face to face with mortality, George decided to give up music completely and go back to college to become a doctor. Quite an audacious plan for a twenty-one-year old rhythm guitar player who rode a *Harley Davidson* Chopper. And guess what? He actually did it, studying medicine in the Dominican Republic and eventually becoming an anesthesiologist himself; mastering the very same medical skills that had nearly killed him. Matthew, as he began to recover, tried his best to get back into playing the bass and I booked a few days in New York's *Record Plant*, trying, without success, to co-produce my second album with the help of Lou Reed's dazzling *Rock and Roll Animal* guitarist Steve Hunter. With *Aquashow* alumni Frank Owens on piano and Rick Marotta on drums. Matthew played his white *Fender Precision* bass and knew his parts well but to my ears at least, the sessions weren't *happening*, weren't as inspiring as I thought they should be. After only a few days, I called it all off. Looking back, I wish I had given Matthew a little more time to heal and had held off on recording until he was fully ready to rock. Today, the rough mixes of those sessions, especially the rhythm track of *Visions of the Night,* sound very good to me but everyone from label to management was clamoring for the new album to get underway and, in a way, you could say I left my brother behind. In the end Matthew did all right for himself, becoming my own tour manager and then working for many successful bands and artists including, most recently, comedian, actor *and* banjo player *Steve Martin*. Actually, you can bet he has made a far better living doing just that than had he remained my bassist. Still it pains me ...

After the accident, and aborted recording sessions, New York was just a place I wanted to escape from so when Paul Rothschild, who had produced both Janis Joplin and *The Doors,* became interested in working with me after Lou Reed became *indisposed,* the idea of spending much of the yuletide season in Los Angeles, pink Christmas trees and all, didn't seem so bad. *RCA Records* liked the idea too and was convinced that Paul was *the guy* to guarantee that their substantial investment in me would pay off. For my part, I was spending RCA's advance as fast as I could and even with my formidable record contract, and the guaranteed royalty advances therein, I was barely keeping up with rent, lifestyle and bad habits. Geraldine and I had upgraded from our nondescript modern high-rise studio and moved into a classy two-bedroom pre-war apartment on East 72nd Street where we had a sweet Irish maid who came by once a week to clean up our substantial mess. Mick Jagger was renting a lovely townhouse just across the street and *Annie Hall* star Tony Roberts was living on the same floor as us. Up on 3rd Avenue was a classy burger joint, *JG Melons,* with my record, *Last of the Rock Stars,* on the jukebox and Bobby, its gregarious host, always ready to skip us to the head of the line to be seated at a prime table where I could chat with A&P grocery heir Huntington Hartford[3].

In 1975 Geraldine and I were living for months at a time at the fabled *Beverly Hills Hotel* in L.A. We were there long enough to actually change rooms three or four times when we grew tired of seeing the same wallpaper each morning when we awoke. One weekend, we drove up the *Pacific Coast Highway* to San Francisco without even checking out, keeping the room charge clock ticking. My feeling was that it was all going to go away some day, so I better get it while I can. Most of the time during those, *self-indulgent* years, I behaved with an upper middle-class politeness, never trashing my room or crashing my cars; any damage I initiated was only directed to myself. Soon after arriving in LA, a record company executive who shall remain nameless, introduced me to a friendly coke dealer who lived down the coast in Marina del Rey, and we made far too many midnight runs to his beach house. When that was inconvenient, he'd *deliver* the goods personally to the studio while I was recording. Not surprisingly, I think my voice sounds slightly *nasal* on *Lost Generation*.

My *Beverly Hills Hotel* room, which was rather modest when compared to the bungalow suites that Donald Trump liked to haunt, was, of course, being paid for by *RCA*, who were willing, I presumed, to foot the bill. When my manager, Dennis Katz, called me a few days into the recording to warn me that I better vacate *toute suite* because the hotel bill was surely going to freak out the RCA accountants, I said, *Nonsense,* and began to list all the valid reasons why I should stay there, which were ... I can't remember. But whatever I said, it must have done the trick because I did spend months at a time in that luxurious hotel with not one phone call ever coming from RCA about the bill. I sat in the *Polo Lounge* eating *Cobb Salads* while gawking at gorgeous actress Jacqueline Bisset at a table just next to mine; I physically bumped into Jack Palance, who towered over me, at the entrance to the hotel restaurant; I ate breakfast in the downstairs coffee shop next to *Godfather* producer Robert Evans, and, I nearly *bumped* into Elizabeth Taylor on the little paths that crisscrossed in the lush gardens behind the hotel that led to the dozen or so cottage suites hidden among the palms. As our paths crossed, Liz and I looked up at each other and it was one of those awkward moments where whatever direction I turned to walk so did she. Finally, Liz looked me in the eye and said, *"You first, darling."* Sexiest directions I ever received in my life.

From the first time I saw its legendary pink facade, *The Beverly Hills Hotel* seemed to me the perfect place for an artist such a myself to dwell; where I might trade in my pale New York decadence for the sun-drenched movie star kind; where however hot the temperature outside might be, the cavernous fireplace in the lobby would always burn brightly. In the mid 1970's, there were still vestiges of the old Hollywood hanging on, not only at *The Beverly Hills Hotel* but also at old school Hollywood restaurants such as *Nate and Al's* and *St. Germain*. The LA music biz tended to prefer the tequila vibe of *Lucy's Adobe*, where there was a signed photo of then (and future) California governor Jerry Brown with his date, singer Linda Ronstadt, hung prominently on the wall; or *Dan Tana's* where you could show up alone, sit at the bar, and soon be recognized by fellow songwriters; all suffering from writer's block and a thirst for tequila and blow. But it was that old Hollywood that fascinated me most, that I still remember; like something out of a 1950's widescreen, *Technicolor* movie, where you might expect to see Rock Hudson and Doris Day singing in harmony through their perfect white capped teeth and lacquered hair under back-lot lit blue skies, cruising in matching *Thunderbirds* (which was actually the car I rented from *Hertz* while I was there), to sleep in matching single beds as the *Hays Code*[4] demanded. Everything in LA seemed to be pink and green, and when you drove through those gracefully curving drives of Beverly Hills and Bel-Air, where the mansions that fronted onto the street alternated motifs from French Chateau to Spanish stucco to Tudor mansion as you passed by. Everything between Hollywood Hills and Malibu seemed to remind you of a TV show or a 1960's surf movie. I fell in love with both the place and the boundless fabulous luxury of it all, and a line or two of cocaine made it all even more fabulous.

And, I suppose subconsciously, what I also really liked about *The Beverly Hills Hotel* and the fine houses that surrounded it, was that it was just a step or two up from the grand *Garden City Hotel* and the 10th Street house of my youth.

LOST GENERATION, PRODUCED BY THE LATE PAUL ROTHSCHILD, would be my first album for *RCA Records*, with Paul practically promising the label that he would deliver a hit from an artist who didn't really fit the mold of the hit-makers of the time, much the same as he had done for *Columbia Records* with Janis Joplin's smash single *Me and Bobby McGee* three years before. I was hoping that my own move from *red* to *black* on my record company's ledgers would not come with the *posthumous* addendum as it had with poor Janis but so far, no needles had entered my arms (and never would) and it looked like I was on *terra firma* to enjoy the fruits of my labor while RCA recouped their contract buyout and advance. In short, they had spent a shitload of money and were impatient to collect while I just wanted to soak in the local culture and write songs about it. Within days of settling into the *Beverly Hills Hotel*, out came my first official LA song called, what else, *Hollywood*:

Hollywood - Hollywood
You shaped my life with a technicolor carving knife and
And now I don't know what to feel
All my emotions are wrapped up reel to reel...

Downtime in the studio, Paul would recount cautionary tales of the *Lizard King* himself: Jim Morrison, drunk out of his mind, directing traffic on La Cienega Boulevard, living in a modest motel with no phone in his room. Late one-night, Paul dug deep into the Elektra Studio vaults and came out with the master tape of the *Doors'* hit *Hello I Love You*. Engineer Fritz Richmond cranked the volume up and man let me tell you, it was like an awe-fucking-inspiring barbaric stomp, part Attila the Hun, part Stravinsky, part Lord Byron. At the time, I wasn't so much into Jim Morrison as I was into Jackson Browne, the most brilliant LA songwriter, and the rest of the outstanding crew of artists on David Geffen's *Asylum Records*. When I met Glen Frey of *The Eagles* and drank with him at *Dan Tana's*[5] with Harry Dean Stanton joining us I thought Glen was a majorly cool dude, who drove an *Austin Healey*, I think; not to mention that his girlfriend at the time was a recent *Playboy Playmate* of the month. Pretty damn impressive and a worthy role model. And for me, the Eagles' *Lying Eyes* is almost up there with *Positively 4th Street* – love that song!

In LA, Geraldine befriended Sandy Gibson, rock publicist extraordinaire, who knew everybody there was to know and everywhere there was to shop on Rodeo Drive. She and Geraldine took Yoga classes in the morning while I worked on song lyrics; getting ready for the evening sessions at nearby *Elektra Studios*. Driving to La Cienega Boulevard in my rented *T-Bird*, sometimes to really *get ready,* I would pick up a bottle of *Johnny Walker Black* and a six-pack of *Coors* to bring to *work,* even detouring to Marina Del Rey to pick up a gram or two of cocaine. On days off, we entertained ourselves as best we could, even buying one of those *Maps to Movie Stars Homes,* sold by sun-tanned *hawkers* with leathery skins, who sat in beach chairs at the entrance to Beverly Hills, searching for Steve McQueen's house. One night while out with Sandy, the three of us were eating at the legendary (everything better be legendary in Hollywood or it has no right to be there) *Canter's Deli* on Fairfax Avenue and ran into Frank Zappa as he was on his way out, heading to his own recording sessions. Sandy knew Frank and I told Frank what a fan I had been of The Mothers of Invention *Freak Out* album, even being un-cool enough to quote one of his own lines right back to him, *Suzy Creamcheese, what's got into you?* Duly complimented, I suppose, he suggested we could drop by later to the *Record Plant West*, where he was recording something (I never found out what). Naturally, we took him up on it.

I have three distinct memories about visiting Frank Zappa at the *Record Plant* that evening. First, with the exception of Frank and his engineer, the studio was empty, no entourage at all besides us; second, his *Marshall Amp* was set up far out in the studio, cranked up to full volume while Frank sat comfortably in the control room, a very long jack connecting his guitar to his amp, probably avoiding ear damage. And third and most surprisingly, when Sandy Gibson lit up a joint he told her to put that thing out *immediately*. Wow! Frank Zappa was straight, in the old sense of the word, meaning that he didn't do drugs. We also visited an *Eagles* session during our stay there as well, and I remember seeing Don Henley sitting on the stairs outside the studio looking exhausted. Unlike with Frank, there were quite an entourage there with the *Eagles*, most of them young, beautiful and female...

The pre-production work for my album was done at Paul Rothschild's house in Laurel Canyon, a large woody cabin that he had designed himself, complete with hidden stashes for hiding drugs. I actually saw him once press a panel in the wall and a drawer came out of nowhere full of pot and rolling papers. When Paul was just starting out as a producer and *The Paul Butterfield Blues Band* album, a band he discovered, was climbing the charts, he got busted on the New Jersey Turnpike for a mere couple of joints and actually went to prison, I believe. So, he was still a bit paranoid and who could blame him? We'd sit around his kitchen table and smoke joints and go over songs and arrangements, deciding what would and wouldn't go on the album. One night, Bobby Neuwirth, who has remained a friend to this day, dropped by and sat at that kitchen table with us. Bobby, not only had the *supporting role* in the Bob Dylan film *Don't Look Back,* when he was working as Bob's tour manager, confidant and point-man, but also co-wrote *Mercedes-Benz*, another posthumous hit for Janis Joplin which Paul produced.

Considering the musicians involved, you could say that the recording sessions for *Lost Generation* at *Elektra Studio* on La Cienega Boulevard deserve a place in rock history. The band not only included ex-Derek and the Dominoes drummer (and co-author of *Layla*) Jim Gordon but also Paul Simon keyboardist Richard Tee and bassist Gordon Edwards of Stuff as well as LA homeboy Ned Doheny (who has a street *Doheny Drive* named after his family) on guitar. When it came time for overdubs, Paul suggested we use two musicians from Louisiana who he had brought to LA: amazing slide guitarist, Sonny Landreth, and vocalist Bobby Kimball, eventually the lead singer of *Toto*. It was Sonny's first session ever as a sideman and when Paul asked him how much he wanted to be paid, Sonny replied with a memorable request, something every musician might keep in mind: *"Can you pay my rent?"*

Word was spreading around LA about those amazing sessions and *LA Times* writer Robert Hilburn stopped by to sample a preview of what the finished album would sound like, which made Paul very nervous as he had never allowed a journalist into one of his sessions before. But no matter how great the band sounded, I was haunted by who *wasn't* there, my brother Matthew, not playing bass, left out in Garden City, still recovering from his car accident injuries, both physical and emotional. I flew Matthew out to LA to visit me for a few days, to witness the sessions, to feel involved in some way, to alleviate my own guilt, but his pain was evident and so was mine. When he returned to New York, even more depressed and demoralized, my mother angrily called me on the phone, told me I was *a terrible person*. Was she right or had I made the only decision possible? In the short term, it seemed obvious that I had to move on without Matthew, but in the long term I wish I had stood my ground and included him in on those sessions. Besides, I think now that bassist Gordon Edwards, in spite of his virtuosity, over-played so much that between him and Jim Gordon's drumming there was little room for my rhythm guitar or even my singing. Matthew's bass playing on *Aquashow*, I now realize, had been instrumental to the groove, much more than anyone realized at the time, maybe there was an embedded DNA *rhythm* between brothers that should have been recognized and nourished.

But when I brought the first mixes back with me to New York, RCA Records, was not as enthralled with the results of those sessions as the *Dan Tana* crowd was, and, at the insistence of A&R head Mike Berniker, Paul Rothschild was asked to remix most of the album. Mike was a nice guy with undeniable arrangement talents who had himself produced many artists with a *similar* style to my own such as

... Perry Como, Steve Lawrence & Eydie Gorme, Johnny Mathis and Barbra Streisand. Get my point? To ensure the final album would come out close to the way RCA had envisioned it, Mike himself flew out to LA along with my manager Dennis Katz and within days was actually going head to head with Paul Rothschild in a shouting match in the studio while I hid under the recording console. A compromise was agreed upon allowing Paul to remix only a few of the tracks if he changed the sequence of the album, putting the slow title song *Lost Generation* first (instead of the fast *Visions of the Night*) because Mike Berniker was big believer that ballads broke solo artists. *Elliott Murphy is not a band!* he kept insisting.

In spite of these difficulties, I think *Lost Generation* was a noble effort and contained a the song which I often open my live shows with today, *A Touch of Mercy*.

I was walking down Main Street just the other day – thinking about Brian Jones and the final getaway – when a man with a collar came to see me saying – son why do you greet me this a way? What I say?

The Brian Jones reference is obvious but the man with a collar was a reference to a minister from the *Garden City Community Church*, who came to visit my bereaved family just days after my father died. He was so full of piety and religious nonsense, that my mother almost literally threw him out of the house, screaming, *"What can you do for me? My husband is dead!"* I don't think she ever voluntarily stepped foot into a church since then.

Another song, *History*, was my only look back at my roots:

Summer in Suburbia – we'd catch fireflies – put them in a jar – and watch them die – you and me baby we could have gone so far – we could have had two cars – and lived a sweet sweet lie.

Is that what I thought about the promise of the American dream? A sweet, sweet lie? I can't say for sure but I can say that I never wanted to return to my roots, never wanted to make it big and buy the biggest house around. That's what Billy Joel and Bruce Springsteen did, they stayed true to their origins, their *homeland* but it wasn't me. No matter how successful I did or did not become I think I would have gone far, far away. Like right to where I am now.

Lost Generation briefly make it into the *Billboard Top 100 Albums* chart and I set out on a promotional club tour with Lou Reed's last band backing me up. We started the tour in the south and I have two distinct memories of Memphis. After the show, I drove out to Graceland, Elvis' home, and tried to convince the guard at the gate to wake up the *King* (although I doubt he was sleeping) because not only was I a fellow RCA artist but my grandfather was from Tupelo, Mississippi, Elvis' home town. But he was under strict orders not to disturb them up at the big house, maybe there was a party going on in the fabled *jungle room* and sent me on my way. My great drummer at the time was named *Mouse,* and he was black and shaved his head clean and I remember him showing up at the soundcheck in a dark mood because a local barber had refused to serve him. Can you believe that? I hope things have changed ...

Hollywood was the single off the album and it enjoyed a regrettably short radio life, probably due to its slowed down spoken introduction:

I remember when you were on the farm – dreaming about Andy Warhol – getting felt up in the barn – and wondering if that's moral.

Or maybe it was because of the sexual innuendos of being *felt up* which in my youth meant getting your hands under a girl's blouse. When you listen to the hip-hop lyrics of today, I can say that things *definitely have changed.* I went out on a promotional tour with a VP from RCA and lunched with radio programmers all over the midwest and we succeeded in getting some decent airplay, but still, the country was not ready for an album which contained the lyrics:

The legless Vietnam survivor – he's trying to find a job or a wife – because he can't find peace with honor – as he gets conditioned to his wheel chair life.

Peace with honor was the *doublespeak* Nixon had used to describe the catastrophic way the Vietnam War had ended; refugees lined up on the roof of the US embassy in Saigon, desperate to board overloaded helicopters, so many *MIA* left behind, a legacy of 50,000 Americans killed, hundreds of thousands of Vietnamese dead, and all for what? But this was almost ten years before Bruce Springsteen's powerful anthem, *Born in the USA,* addressed the subject head-on and either I missed getting my point across or America was not ready to receive it. The album kind of came and went, kindly written off by many East Coast critics to a *sophomore jinx*. Not surprisingly, this record gained more traction on the west coast then the east, and critic Robert Hilburn listed it among his favorite albums of the year. I wanted to shoot the cover with acclaimed LA photographer, Norman Seeff, but Paul Rothschild had some kind of feud going with him, which I never understood. He strongly suggested I find someone else and, *having no horse in this race,* I reluctantly agreed. Finally, maybe it was through Sandy Gibson, I was introduced to Ed Caraeff, another fine LA photographer who at 17 years old had taken the iconic shot of Jimi Hendrix kneeling before his guitar and setting it ablaze during his epic performance at the *Monterey Pop Festival.* Wanting to stay true with my hotel themed cover shots, which had I had begun with at the *Plaza Hotel* with *Aquashow,* I tried to set up a photo session at the *Beverly Hill Hotel,* but that was either forbidden by the hotel management or too expensive for *RCA Records*, whatever, and we finally did the photo session in Ed's own studio where he draped a white parachute as backdrop and I wore my father's *E & M* monogramed cufflinks. The problem was, with the white parachute behind me, it appeared as if there were *otherworldly* beams of light emitting from my *saintly* head; that with my long blond hair and pious, almost beatific, gaze, it was like I was trying to portray some

Just A Story from America

kind of religious icon. Back to Elliott the prophet! In truth, the only real *miracle* that occurred with that album was that somewhere during the transfer of Ed Caraeff's photo to the printer, my eyes had changed color from green to brown.

Lost Generation has outlived its naysayers and not only keeps coming back in CD reissues all over the world but also, in 2015, *Rolling Stone* listed it among the *10 singer-songwriter albums from the 1970's* that they loved at the time and reprinted Paul Nelson's very positive review. As for me, I think it was a fine but flawed album, lyrically more ambitious then the one before but the production didn't always let them shine through. I remember Jim Gordon complimenting me on the songs and my singing but I'm not sure if Richard Tee or Gordon Edwards even had my guide vocals in their headphones. The most satisfying track for me had been *Visions of the Night*, a loping *boogey* and the only track Paul had allowed me to let loose with my harmonica:

Hey baby, now you're all alone – time to think about yourself – there's nobody sitting next to you – drinking to your health ...

As I drove around Hollywood that December with all those pink Xmas trees, I guess that song was the *ghost of Christmas future*[6], talking to me in 1976 ...

Chapter Eight

NIGHT LIGHTS

RCA Studios NYC: Elliott Murphy, Ernie Brooks, Andy Paley & Jerry Harrison 1976

Just A Story from America

Manager Dennis Katz and I, to calm the troubled waters up at *RCA* and make it all right again, formulated a plan to do just that. Get me a one-way ticket on the proverbial *red-eye* flight from LA, leave the *Hollywood* sign withering under the fabled west Coast sunshine where it belongs and bring me home to the nights lights of New York, pronto, while spreading the word to anyone with a vested interest in my career that *the prodigal son has returned*, and is booking serious amounts of time at New York's legendary *Electric Lady Studios*. Dennis' brother guitarist and singer Steve Katz, a fine musician himself, promised to both be sympathetic to my brand of literary rock, while keeping the production *organic*, as he sat behind the glass as designated producer. Also, I set out on a search for musical guests, street-wise musicians still living in the northeast corridor of the republic, which would eventually include not only the *Velvet Underground's* most underrated member, Doug Yule but, most importantly, the most well known Long Island musician to emerge in decades – *Billy Joel!*

My other challenge was to try and put together a dependable band that could both record *and* tour with me, all on a reasonable budget, and bridge the gap between high-priced studio cats and lower-paid road warriors. I started asking around about what happened to the band that had opened for *The New York Dolls* at the *Mercer Arts Center,* on New Year's Eve 1971 - *The Modern* Lovers - and found out that after finally being signed by *Warner Brothers Records* they had gone west to record an album, soon thereafter imploding as leader Jonathan Richmond set out on his own very idiosyncratic musical journey[1]. Long telephone calls soon followed with bassist Ernie Brooks and keyboard player Jerry Harrison who were both *Harvard* graduates with incredible matching curly *lion's mane* hairdos. Ernie and Jerry, were now living back in Boston and I took numerous trips up there with Geraldine in my red MGB convertible, often staying at the *Collonade Hotel* in a suite which overlooked a major thoroughfare that cut right through the heart of the city.

Arriving at the hotel, way after midnight, I sat down in that room and began to write *Drive All Night*[2], a song that continues to work in many different arrangements, slow or fast, solo, duo or full band, including (as I write this) just last night, when I opened my duo show with Olivier Durand on guitar in the tiny village of *Skebobruk*[3], Sweden singing these words:

> *Oh won't you be my night connection – Give me true highway affection – Please don't ask where we're going – I'm trying to race the light – And we can drive all night ...*

Jerry and Ernie steered me toward their pal, handsome Andy Paley[4], as a possible drummer. Andy had the spirit and sense of humor we needed who would keep us laughing on the long drives to come when *RCA* rented us a shiny new Cadillac *Coupe De Ville*, with Matthew, now my tour manager, at the wheel. The four of us rehearsed at *Aerosmith*'s spacious rehearsal hall in Framingham, twenty miles or so outside of Boston on Interstate 90, where blown-out *Marshall* speaker cabinets littered the parking lot, and where we tried to get in shape for both recording and live shows. *William Morris*, my booking agency at the time, came up with the bright idea that we could warm up for recording by going out as the opening act in the most absurd combination of musical styles since Jimi Hendrix opened for *The Monkees*. In a series of shows in northern Canada, we warmed up the frozen crowd, opening for 1950's revival band *Sha Na Na*. To be fair, I must say that the guys in *Sha Na Na* were very cool, treated me and my band royally, and often asking what the hell I was doing with them up there in the *frozen wilderness* on this tour. Everyone recognized that it was an absurd mis-match as I was supposed to be about the future of rock 'n roll and they were a very talented (and funny) 1950's revival show all about the past, that had become famous overnight thanks to their hilarious performance in the *Woodstock* film. I've heard that Bruce Springsteen refused to open for anyone ever again after a tour with the *Chicago*, deciding he'd rather

Just A Story from America

play a half-full club of his own fans than an arena full of folks impatiently waiting for the headliner. A courageous decision which ultimately paid off and which I should have made myself.

When it came time to begin the *Night Lights* sessions, I brought Ernie, Jerry and Andy down from Boston, eventually putting them up at the fabled *Chelsea Hotel,* New York's bohemian mecca on West 23rd Street. First, I had proposed they stay at *The Warwick*, a classy mid-town hotel where *The Beatles* were *barricaded* when they arrived in New York in 1964 and the whole town went nuts, but Jerry and Ernie, both *Harvard* graduates I remind you, thought *The Warwick* way too bourgeoisie for their radical chic taste and preferred to move thirty blocks downtown to the more *authentic Chelsea.* I, of course, obliged convinced they would experience the *bohemian* experience they were looking for, especially when Jerry was startled awake one night when a local hooker and her *john* suddenly entered into his room at the *Chelsea,* after the night clerk gave them the key, thinking the room vacant. Fatefully, after my own *crack-up,* ten years later, thanks to my typing skills, I landed a secretarial gig at the *Chelsea Hotel* for some months, in a curious top floor business located in connecting rooms; a mother and son operation out of a Charles Dickens novel, that sold photo slides of great works of art, long before the internet made it obsolete. In truth, the *Chelsea Hotel* was both cool and artsy with impeccable rock credentials: Janis Joplin and Leonard Cohen had spent long stays there, and Bob Dylan mentioned it in a song. But to be honest, I was never a real bohemian, never attracted to a marginal existence, never seeing the allure in it nor the necessity of being a starving artist in order to create great works of art, for that matter. Blame it on the way I was brought up with a *Cadillac* backseat view of the privileged life that my father was able to provide while he was alive. Downgrading just to spite your parents never made much sense to me, in fact it seemed entirely *unauthentic* even when it became the modus operandi of so many *punks.* If you want to see what the children of the *American Dream* really look like, look at me.

Before recording began I had a fateful meeting with the jovial Ken Glancy, president of *RCA Records* during my tenure on the label. I liked Ken and enjoyed the best relationship I ever had with a major label record company president with him. Maybe it was because we were both Irish and we both liked our *Scotch* on the rocks and early in the afternoon. Ken seemed genuinely concerned after listening to my *Lost Generation* album, that I was going through some sort of depression as the lyrics suggested. At that meeting, we both drank Scotch, him *J&B*, me *Johnny Walker Black*[5], and he tried to cheer me up. *Look around you Elliott, life is good, you're talented and we're behind you.* Ken Glancy was right, of course, and I should have valued our relationship so much more than I did. When I eventually left *RCA* for *Columbia* I didn't even have the decency to call him and tell him first, which I certainly should have. Long after I ran into Ken Glancy on 57th Street totally by chance and with much chagrin I took that opportunity to make amends, telling him that the way I had left the label, letting my lawyers and managers do the dirty work, was not right and that I was truly sorry for that after all that he had done for me, that I should have gone to see him first, man to man. Ken was a classy guy, ever the gentleman, and he was forgiving and friendly and with a sly wink told me to keep an eye on my overseas royalties from RCA as I had sold more albums in France than I probably realized. *France?* I asked. Never heard anything about it...

Back to *Night Lights* where the pressure was on for me to come up with some genuine hit songs. The trouble was that I *thought* I had written a few hits already and was at a loss as to why they hadn't climbed the charts[6]. It was hard for me to understand how I might change my writing style to fit the format of FM radio of the day. Was I even *capable* of changing in such a way? I mean, wasn't *Last of the Rock Stars* as generationally significant as Don Mclean's *American Pie?* Was not *How's the Family* as poignant as Janis Ian's *17?* And tell me that the chorus of *Hollywood* is not as catchy as the Kinks' *Celluloid heroes?* I went back to my *Wurlitzer* electric piano with a renewed sense of purpose, staring out the window of my East 72nd

Street apartment where the huge luminous *RCA* sign, set atop the corporate headquarters, beckoned in the distance, something akin to the green light at the end of the dock in *The Great Gatsby*. The *night lights* of Manhattan were arrayed before me, like sparkling distant jewels, and just as Brian Wilson had put his piano in a sandbox to feel the beach between his toes, I put my piano next to the window and let those seductive lights work their magic. Like the sirens in *Ulysses*, they called out to me.

Somewhere in these night lights lies the answer, I wrote down first, not knowing where the song was heading but beginning what was to become the chorus of *Diamonds by The Yard*, the opening cut of that album. I was a moderately talented piano player at best, but this song, being in the key of C, *the people's key,* flowed easily down from my head to my hands on the keyboard. It was a three–chord special, as simple in structure as *Louie, Louie* or *Twist and Shout*, its energy slowed down in the same fashion as the city itself come the *wee-wee* hours. My inspiration, as absurd as it might sound, was Gershwin's *Rhapsody in Blue*, only this time as a rock ballad with a soaring guitar lead, overdubbed in glorious three-part harmony at the finish. My artistic code would be embedded in the chorus' refrain:

Midnight I surrender – I leave beneath your ancient spell – you've been my lover since I can't remember – you saved my life with the stories you tell…

At the time *Tiffany & Co.* had come out with a new piece of Jewelry, a diamond strung necklace designed by Elsa Peretti, and she had called it *Diamonds by the Yard*. Seeing an ad for it in *The New Yorker*, I knew right away that I had found the song title for my homage to Manhattan, my magical *Land of Oz*, its dazzling night lights brightening the night sky above, its subterranean crisscrossed by subway tunnels, its soul, both tough and tender, permanently a part of my own to this day.

More songs came quickly after that, as I had a concept for my writing. The same as I looked out of my 26th floor window upon New York, this album would be a nocturnal view of my love affair with rock and roll. *Looking for a Hero* (which was to be the first single off the album), contained what I believe to be the most prophetic lines I ever wrote, as rock 'n roll seems to be entering its own dark ages, unheard on the radio, totally decimated by the march of *hip-hop*:

A thousand years – explore the ruins – a tour guide explains bubble gum chewing – they had religion skyscraperism – if you were black you lived in prison – through ancient billboards we've been told – they had one god – his name was Rock 'n Roll...

For the *coda* of *Looking for a Hero*, Doug Yule and Steve Katz worked up a very *Velvet Underground* like refrain that I quickly wrote in the studio: *Looking for a soul – look in rock 'n roll*. And that says it all.

And also I was not afraid to write about my struggles with my own personal demons in *You Never Know What You're In For*:

Getting late they were spaced just a trace of the old coming down - Ancient fun one and one he said someday we'll leave this town - but magazines glamour scenes in betweens had him nailed to the ground - And the sounds still waiting to be found...

There is also a song on *Night Lights*, called *Lady Stilletto* and you might note that "stiletto" is misspelled and that with the extra T added it's an anagram for *St Elliott* because I meant that song as a sort of homage to poet Patti Smith but also to myself. It was my attempt to exaggerate Patti's punk persona in the *grand guignol* style of, say, a Robert Crumb comic. I wanted to say we were two artists sharing the same vision but I'm not sure if I succeeded, at least not with her. I had been a fan of Patti Smith since her slim book of poetry *Seventh Heaven* came out in 1972, containing poems with titles such as *Edie Sedgwick* and *Marianne Faithfull* and even mentioning fellow blond ex-Stones *Brian Jones,* a once fashion role model for me. Patti had started playing gigs with rock-journalist, and all-around good guy, Lenny Kaye, backing her on guitar. When I saw them perform in a near empty club at *The Performance Center* in Cambridge, Massachusetts, while I was selling out next store, I became convinced that I was the one to produce her and give her career a needed boost. Back in New York, I contacted Ray Sicala, manager of *The Record Plant* studios, who offered me some free studio time to demo the project if so needed. But when I called Patti she wasn't interested, hardly gave me the time of day in spite of my enthusiasm for her work, and when she signed with Clive Davis' new label *Arista,* she chose to work with producer John Cale. I can't really say with any certitude if Patti ever heard *Lady Stilletto,* but my instinct tells me that if she did, she didn't appreciate it in the spirit I meant it, because since then, every time I've seen her she barely acknowledges my presence. So be it. On the other hand, I've had two songs written about me, and although there are some strange lines in both, I can only say I'm honored. But that's just me.

Ernie, Jerry, Andy and I went into *Electric Lady Studios* Studio B and cut three tracks; *Diamonds by the Yard, Never as old as you,* and *Lady Stilletto.* Although RCA liked my new material and the *organic sound* of Steve Katz, they wanted more finesse, more musicianship, a bit of commercial polish even, and as I was in agreement with them, I had to let Jerry and Andy go, which was both difficult and painful because I liked these two guys so much. But in retrospect, me letting them go might have been the best thing that ever happened to either of them because Jerry Harrison, soon after leaving me, joined the *Talking Heads* and Andy, who adored *The Beach Boys,* became Brian Wilson's producer for a while. So, as Lou Reed once said to me, *things worked out okay after all, didn't they?*

The remaining seven tracks on *Night Lights* were recorded with a stellar team of players including jazz legend Richard Davis on stand-up bass for *You Never Know What You're in For,* a song I've played thousands of times in concert ever since. But for me, the high-point came when my Long Island buddy Billy Joel came down to play piano on *Deco Dance*. I knew Billy all the way back from his days in a local Long Island band, *The Hassles*; they had even played at my father's restaurant *The Sky Club* in 1966, the last year of its existence. Billy and I went way back both generationally and geographically; both of us born in 1949, both of us growing up on Long Island, both of us playing in the same *joints* honing our chops, back in a pre-*YouTube* era when that was still possible. One snowy night in 1968, I remember seeing Billy's band *The Hassles* playing in a forgotten Syosset rock club, *My House*. Even though I got into a car accident on the way there, skidding off the slippery exit of the *Long Island Expressway* and crushing the bumper of my mother's Chevy Impala convertible[7], I still made it to the show. *The Hassles* had a good reputation on Long Island, already in the same league with local heroes such as *The Vagrants, The Illusion, The Good Rats* and *The Rich Kids*. They opened their set with their version of *The Spencer Davis Group's* all-time party anthem, *Gimme Some Lovin'* and goddamn if it wasn't note for note perfect with Billy both singing the lead and playing the iconic riff on his *Hammond B3* Organ. Even then, I knew that boy was bound for stardom.

SPOKEN MUSICAL INTRODUCTIONS TO ROCK SONGS HAD GONE out of style long ago, maybe the last memorable ones being *The Countours Do you love me* and Dion's *Runaround Sue*, that I had sung to those girls in a Garden City basement when I was in Junior High School. But regardless of current music trends, I put one on the opening of *Hollywood* and now I wanted to do the same thing again on *Deco-Dance*, a kind of *faux* Ragtime mid-tempo number on the dangers of a short-lived celebrity.

One way or another – they're gonna get you soon – they're gonna crush your banana – they're gonna blow your balloon – One way or another

Just A Story from America

– your face is gonna fall – but you'll still smile in your river – you'll just be a little wet – baby that's all!

Deco Dance was another song written on that magical *Wurlitzer* electric piano, where my muse came to visit the moment I turned it on and which I only wish I had today. As soon as it was finished, I knew this had to be the song on *Night Lights* that Billy Joel would play on. At the time, Geraldine and I were friendly with both Billy and his then wife/manager Elisabeth as we all lived near-by on New York's Upper East Side, even celebrating Christmas Eve ensemble one year. I have a memory of showing up at their apartment once, to meet up for dinner, and Billy while sitting at the piano, telling me he was just back from somewhere and was working on a song called *New York State of Mind* and singing the intro to me, *Some folks like to get away* ... But when I reminisced with Billy about this time a few years ago at his house in Palm Beach, he said it was impossible because he was sure he wrote that song somewhere else. Well, I don't know whose memory is in better shape, both of us being veterans of the *rock 'n roll wars,* and I don't dare dispute Billy's version of when he wrote his own song, but for now I'm going to stick with my own recollections. Or as my brother Matthew likes to say, *never let the truth get in the way of a good story.*

I *can* say, with confidence and accuracy, that when Billy Joel came down one evening to *Electric Lady Studios* to lay down his piano part on *Deco Dance,* it was as close to a perfect one-take, no sweat session as I have ever experienced in all my career. He was truly amazing, learning the song, chord changes and arrangement, during the *run-through* and sounding as close to the *King of Ragtime Scott Joplin* as the song allowed; his playing giving the song an uplifting mood in spite of the cautionary tale contained in the lyrics. Billy's bopping rhythm really made the whole thing swing and once, while out at a bar-b-que at my then manager Steve Leber's house in Cedarhurst, Long Island, I was thrilled as I watched his wife and a dozen of her five-towns[8] friends perform a perfectly synchronized suburban version of a *line dance* to the song, something they had worked out just for my visit. I was truly grateful as it was rare that I saw people actually dancing to my records and this song connected big-time with a genuine Long Island crew of babes. Billy would have been proud if he was there.

I was imagining a very different sort of dance when I wrote *Isadora's Dancers*, inspired by watching the Vanessa Redgrave film *Isadora*[9], but there was also a connection to Geraldine and my time in San Francisco as well, maybe thinking back to that topless dancer we lived with and her lonely daughter, who spent her days in front of the TV.

I've gone to meet Isadora's dancers – wrote that girl on her own blue jeans – I've given up trying to find the answer – and these times – they're sure turning mean...

For the arrangement, I wanted to give *Isadora's Dancers* a sense of lost innocence and Steve's suggestion of adding a non-professional children's chorus was an inspired idea. One bright autumn afternoon, a yellow school bus parked in front of *Electric Lady Studios* and out poured the 4th grade class of Dennis Katz' daughter for a *field day* outing at a genuine rock 'n roll studio. They were wonderful and even uplifting for a fairly *down* song, and I promised myself that in some future recording I would again use children's voices which is exactly what I did on my next album which featured the *Saint Paul's Boys Choir* singing beautifully on *Anastasia*. Isadora Duncan and Anastasia Romanov, historic women both, surrounded by a chorus of angelic voices. What shocks me today is to think that most of those kids who sang that day are well in their fifties by now!

The album received a stellar review in Rolling Stone (the last one Paul Nelson would write himself) and two singles (*Looking for a Hero* and *Manhattan Rock*) got heavy airplay in both Cleveland and New York. But the sales were lagging and I was easily lured away from *RCA* when *Columbia Records* came calling. Once again, the new label blaming my lack of sales on the last label's mishandling of radio promotion etc. But I was always wondering why my music was not clicking with a larger public. In fact, that still puzzles me.

∼

GERALDINE AND I HAD BECOME GOOD BUDDIES WITH ARMA Andon, who was a *Columbia* VP, and his then wife the late Libet Johnson, heiress to the *Johnson & Johnson* fortune. For a few short years, our adventures with Arma and Libet were literally the stuff American dreams are made of: long sunset cocktail hours at *Trader Vics,* located in the *souterrain* of the *Plaza Hotel,* where we sipped strong rum concoctions with tiny paper umbrellas helping us float into oblivion; sumptuous dinners in Libet's floor-through 5th Avenue apartment with *Papa's* late granddaughter, model Margaux Hemingway, where the elevator opened right onto her vestibule and a lovely Mary Cassett painting hung on the wall above a large bowl of Beluga caviar; and, summering in the guesthouse of their Quogue estate, where I wrote some of the songs for *Just A Story from America.* Come July and August weekends, the driveway there would be littered with *Mercedes* and *BMWs* (I thought my MGB was the coolest *ride* around), as overflowing *Gatsby*-like parties went on late into the wee hours, and other Columbia artists such as ex-*Traffic* member Dave Mason would come out to party. One July weekend, we sailed up the Atlantic Coast, from New York to Maine, in Libet's late brother's ocean-going sailing yacht, *The Sea Prince,* and docked into Freeport, Maine, home of *LL Bean,* where my cousin Tom Sidar worked as a company executive. I think Tom was stunned when he saw the huge yacht pull into the harbor. *It's not mine baby!* were my first words after disembarking.

That life-style was both thrilling and undeniably privileged and I don't apologize for enjoying my short lived *Nick Carraway*[10] vantage point; there were magic moments too memorable and historic to ever forget such as sitting ringside for the 1976 Muhammad Ali – Ken

Norton heavyweight fight at Yankee Stadium or watching George Plimpton's Fireworks display from a yacht in Quogue. But still, I was often plagued by doubts if *squatting* in the lap of luxury was where I should be at that point in my musical career. It was cushy but was it rock 'n roll? Shouldn't I have been spending more time out on the road, playing any club that would book me, perfecting my craft, getting so comfortable that the stage was my second home? Unfortunately, nobody but me saw it that way and it wasn't until I left the world of the major labels and started touring Europe regularly that I really became a seasoned performer. Better late than never. Also, that sort of conspicuous consumption was still a *no-no*, for the lingering sixties mentality, although personally I saw no reason why rock 'n rollers needed to play down their wealth. Didn't John Lennon ride around in a psychedelic *Rolls Royce?* Once, when *RCA* complained about the sales of *Night Lights,* I suggested they release a limited edition inside a *Louis Vuitton* cover at a premium price and they thought I was kidding. Hate to say it, but I was proven right about flaunting it if you got it, because today the most successful *hip-hop* artists proudly dress in *Gucci, Saint Laurent and Dior*, ride around in *Ferraris, Maybachs* and *Lamborghinis* and brag about an over-the-top luxurious life style in their raps. But all that's in my distant past now, my life-style is comfortable but far from luxurious and Libet Johnson, a lovely woman, generous and kind, passed away from early on-set Alzheimer's Disease while still in her 50's. I always wanted to tell her that she had inspired a song on *Night Lights,* a waltz that I still play when I grow nostalgic and my thoughts return to those heady days. It's called *Rich Girls:*

Rich girls smoke Kools - Flirt with hesitation - Can I please help you - Cries servants with vacations - And leaves me with a vision - Southampton gazebo - Is my left wing disturbing your senses - and I'm left with your pink dress pretensions - That's all...

∼

Chapter Nine

A YANKEE IN QUEEN ELIZABETH'S COURT

Rolling Stone Ad "Just A Story From America" 1977

When Matthew and I came back from Europe in 1972, decked out in our brand new Kings Road *threads*, the last vestige of *Swinging London*[1], including my python-skin boots and *mellow yellow* velvet pants, and strutted into *Max's Kansas City*, owner Mickey Ruskin right away seated us in the preferred back room because he figured we must be *somebody important,* which, of course, we actually weren't. That was the thing about *Max's*, where it was possible to instantly reinvent yourself as a *superstar* in that micro-galaxy of macro-egos, if you dressed, talked and walked the part; Andy Warhol's fifteen minutes of fame waiting to be illuminated under a Dan Flavin *fluorescent bulb* work of art. Coming from exotic far-off London, where we had been among the first humans to down cheeseburgers and milk shakes at the original *Hard Rock Café* right off of Hyde Park.

When I signed with *Columbia Records* in 1976, I had a valid case for returning to London, the city where so many great records were born. My initial plan was to record at *Beatles'* producer George Martin's *AIR Studios* or *Olympic* where the Stones often recorded, and I actually met Sir George himself, who couldn't have been more charming, at a *CBS Records*[2] *International convention*. At that same convention, I ran into ex-*Rolling Stones* guitarist Mick Taylor and asked him if he would agree to play on a track if I ever did record in London. Mick seemed interested, so I quickly got to work on a song that would fit his slide playing; thinking of all the rock ballads that had soothed my trouble soul:

When the moon was just right – we could turn off the light and just listen – pray to the night – hold on so tight – you could hear crystal stars as they glisten – lovers in vain like to walk in the rain – like to hear a distant train's emotion – and a late radio played very low – no one must know this devotion ...

The verses came like automatic writing because the story was so clear in my head but when it came time for the chorus I was at a loss. With deadlines looming, I settled on a generic theme, a sort of homage to all the slow songs that had moved my heart and soul. Songs like Otis Redding's *I've Been Loving You Too Long*, Dylan's *Vision of Johanna*, even Percy Faith's *Theme from a Summer Place*.

Rock Ballad – Rock Ballad – Baby and I could listen all night long – to a real slow song – until my tears were gone ...

While in London, I was persuaded to meet with engineer Robin Cable who had worked at *Trident Studios* and was *transitioning* to become a real producer himself. Robin's credentials were very impressive; not only engineering Elton John's *Your Song* but also one of my all-time favorite singles *You're So Vain* by the beautiful Carly Simon, a song which, for a while, got the whole world guessing who the man in question was - Mick Jagger or Warren Beatty. My thinking was that after three albums, I should know my way around the studio well enough to produce my own records if I only had a really great engineer to help me get the sounds in my head down on tape. But *Columbia* insisted that *someone* with the actual title of producer had to be involved in the project before they'd start paying the studio bills and thus Robin was engaged with the implied understanding that we would actually co-produce the album with both our hands on the wheel, so to speak, when it came to the creative direction. Robin could choose the studio and find the musicians we needed while coming up with British arrangers to provide the strings and vocal chorus we needed. My management liked Robin because he didn't ask for too much money and my record company liked him because he was, well, *British*, with a track record of hits, and I liked him because he came from *Trident Studios,* where David Bowie had recorded *Hunky Dory*.

Determined to incorporate lavish orchestration on this album, even if it was something I had avoided in the past, I knew London was the place to do it where payment scale for classical musicians was more reasonable then in New York or LA. My goal was to make a sweeping musical statement, something truly classic and memorable, with this batch of new songs and my recording history trajectory had taken me from New York to Los Angeles and then back to New York again, so it was time to look the other way, across the ocean. With producer, studio and musicians solidly booked, I took off for London in the fall of 1976, traveling again on *Pan Am*, totally psyched. I was on my way to record my first album for *Columbia Records*, finally on the *best* label, armed with a dozen new songs and three guitars: my 1961 Fender *Stratocaster* (which I still have), a sunburst *Les Paul Custom* (can't remember what happened to that one), and my *Gibson J200* acoustic, which sits in its case just steps from where I'm writing. I had no idea as I sat on the plane to London, not the slightest clue, that the resulting album, *Just A Story from America,* would be my swansong to the world of the major labels, and that I'd soon be divorced, broke and sleeping on a cot in my mother's dining room.

I REMEMBER TAKING A WHITE STRETCH LIMO TO JFK AIRPORT, Geraldine and I huddled in the rear, driving through Brooklyn on our way to JFK Airport and finishing off a vial of cocaine before dropping some *Valium* once we took our seats in the first-class cabin. This was not the way my grandfather Murphy had done it when he travelled in the opposite direction sixty-four years before, probably 3rd class in a crowded steamer, full of *your tired, your poor, your huddled masses yearning to breathe free.* I'm ashamed of that but at the same time that's about how every artist I knew of that era was traveling – first class and too stoned to enjoy it. All I was really sure of was that I was *yearning* in the worst way to finally record a hit album, get out of debt and get onto the *Billboard* charts. It was a fortuitous time to be in London; the dollar was riding high against the English Pound and Geraldine and I could justify spending even more money we didn't have. I mean, how many cashmere sweaters can you buy before it gets redundant? I was also chain-reading Raymond Chandler novels such as *The Long Goodbye, Farewell my Lovely,* just about anything with his name on it; even quoting him on the eventual inner sleeve for that album, *you can never know too much about the shadow line and the people who walk it.* That line, which jumped out at me, should have been a warning because the truth was that *I* was the one walking the shadow line about to fade into the shadows. I had left my last real band back in the USA without even telling them where I was going, something my faithful friend and bassist Ernie Brooks loves to remind me of today. But the irony of all this is that however I was suffering personally, even as my bad habits grew, I was still thriving artistically, and this album would contain some of my best songwriting and most mature melodies. What's that all about?

Most of the songs on *Just A Story from America* originated out in Quogue, Long Island where the summer before, Geraldine and I had stayed in a small rented cottage located next to the mansion of Libet and Arma. Weekdays, I stayed out there alone, downing a six-pack of *Coors Beer* for dinner and swimming morning laps in the pool to cure my hangover enough to start writing songs. I took long walks by the nearby beach, hoping I might run into neighbor Budd Schulberg, author of the *The Disenchanted,* a thinly veiled novel based on his time working with F. Scott Fitzgerald when he lived in Hollywood. I never did meet Budd Schulberg but that was the perfect word for my mood at the time: *disenchanted.* There would be two notable exceptions to the Quogue songs, *Anastasia,* which I wrote in London and later became a hit in France, and the title track, *Just A Story from America,* which came to life in the middle of the recording sessions while jamming with drummer Phil Collins who, by the way, was one of the funniest musicians I ever worked with.

The boutique hotel I stayed at while working in London was classy and discreet enough to be a favorite of visiting rock stars endowed with a generous enough recording budget: *The Montcalm,* just off *Marble Arch* with splendid rooms and late-night room service, not far from *AIR Studios* on Oxford Street where the sessions would begin and where I saw Eric Burdon from *The Animals* the day I checked in. I didn't tell him that *House of the Rising Sun* had changed my life, but I took it as a good sign nonetheless. My desire to go to London because of the great sounding records coming from there at the time was legitimate, but also, I had a desperate need to escape from New York, where temptations were high, and work was too often left on the back burner to overcook when cocaine, booze and partying competed for my attention. As for my marriage to Geraldine, let me just say that when cocaine comes in the door love usually goes out the window. By now, I was drinking on a daily basis and that usually led to a call to the *coke dealer of the stars*.[3] And then, after a two-day binge, I'd be popping *Valium*, my heart pounding, desperate to get to sleep. Many afternoons I found myself sitting alone at the piano in a drab midtown rehearsal hall for hours just trying to clear my mind and get on with it. I was in a similar bind to what poor F. Scott Fitzgerald and his unstable wife Zelda must have been in when they left New York for Paris in the 1920's, when even with the constraints of Prohibition, the booze was flowing weekday and weekend. Just as Fitzgerald went to Europe to write *The Great Gatsby*, I went to London to write and record *Just A Story from America*.

Early in my stay, in Winter 1976, when my room service breakfast arrived at my *Montcalm* suite, on the tray, along with scones and Earl Gray tea, was a British tabloid newspaper with the headline, *New Anastasia Found!* Who knows why, but I was drawn to the article. What intrigued me was not that some aged dowager was claiming to be the long-lost daughter of Czar Nicholas Romanov, but why the story of the Russian royal family, gunned down by Bolshevik thugs in a basement room, was still so moving, so tragic, so unnecessary. I picked up my *Gibson J200* guitar, strummed a C chord and started to sing:

Anastasia please come home – your family is on the telephone – they know they left you all alone - with your royalty ... the jewels and the lights of those winter nights and a little girl's eyes oh so wide – I'm not saying they were wrong to fight but I know they were wrong to despise – the joy in a little girl's eyes ...

Anastasia was nearly finished before I took my first sip of tea; one of those songs that came to me whole, like a loaf of bread, all I had to do was to figure out where to cut the slices – verses, choruses and bridge – and put it back together again. Like I said, God works in mysterious ways because if I hadn't read that article in that newspaper that day and written that song which helped establish me in France, I wouldn't be here now, in Paris, recalling it all so clearly. We orchestrated the song with the heavenly *St. Paul's Boys' Choir* and they sang like angels. My dream was to perform *Anastasia* in Moscow some day and that hasn't happened ... yet. But in the late eighties, before the disintegration of the USSR, I was playing a show in Lausanne, Switzerland, at a cross-cultural rock event and on the bill was a young Russian rock band. I put *Anastasia* into my set and sang it with intensity, directing it toward the Russian rockers who sat nearby and listened. Later that night, I asked them what they thought of the song. *Great!* they all said, bobbing their heads in approval. *Very nice ballad! But as Russians,* I asked, *didn't a song about Anastasia have any special meaning for you?* They looked from one to another until finally the leader of the band spoke. *Who is Anastasia?* He asked me.

They had never heard about her, had never been taught about the murder of the Czar. Songs may be written by the *sensitive,* but history is written by the winners. In his *Village Voice* review of the album, Robert Christgau made fun of the song, like *only I* would choose to write a song on such an irrelevant subject in today's world. Personally, I think he was wrong, I think the murder of the Czar's family doomed the Russian Revolution from the start. Even Marie Antoinette was given a trial.

One evening, as I was waiting in the elevator of the *Montcalm* to ascend to my room, singer Stevie Nicks entered, talking briskly with a friend, not noticing me standing in the rear. Beautiful and immensely talented, Stevie was by then a member of the reborn, rebranded and phenomenally successful *Fleetwood Mac,* you could even say she was the media *face* of the band with her *gypsy queen* style of dress a widely copied fashion statement. *Fleetwood Mac* had restarted their stalled career big-time when their second eponymous[4] album shot to number one in 1975. When I was with *Polydor,* they suggested we call the album *The Murphy's,* but I nixed that idea because *Polydor* had already signed Stevie Nicks and Lindsay Buckingham who put out a fine album at around the same time as *Aquashow* under their own family names, *Buckingham Nicks.* I take a tiny part of the credit for Stevie and Lindsay's humongous triumph as the new *Fleetwood Mac* because when they were on Polydor I heard that they complained that I was getting all the media attention, which to their mind, some of which at least, should have gone to them. Disgruntled, they both moved to LA, morphed into Fleetwood Mac members and achieved a success most of us can only dream of.

In 1976, dandy singer-songwriters in aqua colored fur coats were completely out of synch with what was happening in London at the time. The punks were about to claim their place in the spotlight and when the *Sex Pistol's* Johnny Rotten said *Fuck,* live on a BBC television talk show it was a major news event. Ironically, it was *Sex Pistols* mastermind manager Malcolm McLaren who advised me to move to Paris when I met him at *Le Palace* after my 1982 show there. *Why?* I asked. *Beause it's the only place for a poet,* said Malcolm with assurance. In 1990, after moving here, I ran into him again, this time eating in a *rive gauche* bistro. *I took your advice,* I told him, *I moved to Paris.* And I can tell you he seemed pleased. Managers love when artists do what they tell them to do!

Robin Cable proved to be more than a guy who just pushes control board faders around and his contributions to that album, both in sound and arrangements and putting together the studio band, which included *Genesis* leader Phil Collins on drums, have helped enormously. *Progressive Rock* had never been on my personal playlist, and I didn't know much about *Genesis*, but Phil Collins, in spite of my initial skepticism, was a surprisingly good choice to play drums on that album and a blast to work with, always cracking me up. From talking with him, my sense was that Peter Gabriel had left Genesis somewhat abruptly, and I remember during a tea break asking Phil what they were going to do for a lead singer now. He replied that he was so sick of auditioning singers that he might just start singing himself, which is exactly what he eventually did with incredibly successful results, both for *Genesis* and particularly on his solo albums. The only outside musician I brought into the sessions myself was Mick Taylor, the man who quit the Rolling Stones. He carried his own *Ampeg* guitar amp into the studio, told me it had been a present from Keith Richards, and just that alone was enough to impress me. Mick's first slide guitar take on the song during the run-through was the best, of course, but as is often the case we didn't record it! But he got 90% there again on the next take and I was un-Stoneslike *satisfied*, being pretty sure that *Rock Ballad* was the first song he played on after leaving the Stones. That alone counts for a mention in the rock history books.

Geraldine and I ate tasty dinners at *Mr. Chow's* in Knightsbridge and, thanks to Robin, I got to hang out a bit with Harry Nilsson, who wore a fine tweed suit like Sherlock Holmes, and charming Derek Taylor, the celebrated *Beatles* publicist. My take on the town was that if you were a rock star *aristocrat* with a *Bentley*, belonging to a posh men's club on Berkley Square, it was a fine place to live. But I knew I would never fit into that category. English rock stars have the advantage of being born into a pretty defined class system and are schooled how to behave when fame and fortune arrives, and you rise above the *wankers* but for us Americans your bank account defines your class and that's about it.

Recording went fine as we jumped from one great studio to another; George Martin's *AIR* on Oxford Street to *Audio International* to *Marquee*, which was located in the back room of the *Marquee Club* where both *The Who* and *The Rolling Stones* had played gigs early in their career. One untypical morning session at *Marquee* began when in marched the St. Paul's Boys Choir, dressed in their British school boy uniforms, short pants and caps, looking like they should be in *AC/DC*, ready to sing on *Anastasia*. I didn't know what to expect as these kids poked each other with pencils and seemed to enjoy causing general havoc before choir director Barry Rose quickly pulled them into line and in just a few takes they performed the most angelic backing choir you could imagine this side of paradise. Honestly, if there is one recording of mine that I wouldn't change a thing, it's *Anastasia*, from Phil Collins penetrating drums to the boys choir, it was all perfect.

And to give *Just A Story From America* a totally authentic London vibe, I pushed *Columbia* to hire photographer David Bailey to shoot the cover. David was the purported model for actor David Hemming's detached Dionysian character in Michelangelo Antonioni's 1966 film *Blow-Up*, had been married to my favorite French actress, Catherine Deneuve, and had a reputation as brilliant but difficult to work with. He must have been expensive but for me there could be no other choice as David had been responsible for the photos on so many *Rolling Stones* covers and my friend, *Hawkwind* manager Doug Smith, was able to connect us while I convinced Columbia to foot the bill. Doug, Geraldine and I went to David's hidden studio where he kept us waiting for close to an hour before emerging with his camera and beginning the shoot. Months later, he sent to New York, just two dazzling photos, one color – one black and white - although we must have shot hundreds at his studio. For the cover, I chose the black and white shot of me nearly falling off the frame, apropos for my interior life, and for the inner sleeve the lush color head shot. Talented *Columbia* in-house designer Paula Scher used a minimal red and blue lettering for the title on a stark white background and, I've got to say, I think it's one of the best covers of my catalog. *Just A Story from America* was the album of a future expat American artist; red, white and blue cover, like a flag raised over the US embassy in a foreign land.

Just A Story from America

In 2006, an exhibition about my career was staged at the *Mairie of Paris' 6th Arrondisement*[5] and I contacted David Bailey, wanting to know if he could possibly loan us a few outtakes from that photo session to be included in the exhibition. In my email I explained what a thrill it had been to work with him and how that photo had gone on to achieve almost iconic status among my fans. His rather succinct reply was just two words. "No – sorry." Blow-up indeed! But still a brilliant photographer who put the final touch on an album some call classic and I'm proud of to this day. I had played most of the instruments myself including guitars (with the exception of Mick Taylor), *Farfisa* organ, marimba, harmonica, tambourine, harmonium and even Robin's own Portuguese guitar thanks to Robin's wife Tina who came from Portugal on the intro of *Caught Short in the Long Run*, the last song on the album, which like a fly caught in amber showed exactly where I was at the time:

And tonight when they come I'll say they can't see you no more – 'Cause they'll draw out your life through a fine silver straw - And if I was a hero I would have fought them off at your door - But the lines we have drawn and the sides we have chose - And my own indecision how badly that shows - And, God damn, if I was a hero I would have kept our little world closed ...

The Aqua colored *yak* fur coat I'm wearing on the cover had been bought at the *Revillon* boutique at Saks Fifth Avenue with some record company advance. I had immediately fallen in love with it as it looked like something Brian Jones might have sported on *Between the Buttons*. But in 1985, as I was literally and figuratively cleaning up my act and going through my closets, taking stock of my wardrobe, my second wife Rita talked me into donating this magical garment, a remnant from an age when rock stars dressed the part, to the *Salvation Army* charity. A mistake I regret to this day, but I wonder who's wearing it now?

Columbia loved the album but, and this is a big but, they didn't hear an obvious single. Never mind, they were still willing to go full speed ahead with promotion and tour support. When I heard this, alarms should have gone off in my head. *The label doesn't hear a single!* And we should have delayed the release until I could write and record *the* song that everybody would agree was a viable hit single. Apparently, a similar situation arose with Bruce Springsteen when he presented the songs for *Born in the USA* to his manager Jon Landau, who, in a similar fashion, didn't think any of these songs, as great as they were, was an obvious single that could immediately be played on the radio. What was different in Bruce's case, was that after first telling Jon to go write it himself if that was the case, Bruce went back up to his room and wrote *Dancing in the Dark*, a huge hit single which opened the door for the rest of the album to be played on the radio as well.

Columbia Records launched an ad campaign for *Just A Story from America*, centered around a full-page *Rolling Stone* ad which showed me in a pose similar to that on the cover photo[6] anchored with the immortal words, *He could have written a book, but he chose rock 'n roll instead.* Jeez! It sounded like music was my second choice. *Drive All Night* was the single from the album, even if everyone could not agree it *was* a single, and I put together a band in New York of some very difficult UK musicians, now living in the U.S., who after a month or so on the road I couldn't stand to be on the same stage with. We opened for Jeff Lynne's *Electric Light Orchestra* in twenty-thousand seat arenas all across the South and then I called the whole damn thing off. *Columbia* was not thrilled with my move because they had already ordered a giant billboard which would advertise the album on Sunset Strip when I played in LA, but I was desperately unhappy. My brother Matthew, who was my tour manager and had better sense then I, begged me to keep going regardless of how I felt about the band. Just get through it! He was right of course, and I should have listened to him. When you break show business rule #2, *the show must go on,* you pay a heavy price.

The band I had put together were talented enough individually,

Just A Story from America

but never showed me any respect as the band leader, thinking they were bigger stars then me, I suppose. On drums was Jerry Shirley, ex-*Humble Pie* and I made the ridiculous mistake of letting him have a drum solo, totally incongruous with my style of show. On keyboards was the late Peter Woods, who co-wrote the monster hit *Year of the Cat* with Al Stewart who, for the most part, was cool although he liked to rock his *Hammond* organ, nearly tipping it over on stage, which was disconcerting as I was standing next to it. My biggest problem was with guitarist Les Nichol who over-played on every song, but I blame that on myself as well because, with the exception of Mick Taylor's solo on *Rock Ballad*, I had played all the guitars on *Just A Story from America*, and what I really needed was a solid rhythm guitarist not a virtuoso. But these three English guys came as a unit, all for one and one for all, and as time was running out, I regrettably signed them on for the tour too quickly. The one exception was left-handed bassist Larry Russel who had played with Billy Joel and never caused a problem, sang well, and was the only *reasonable* member of the band. A few years later, when I took a band to France to do a tour with Irish blues legend Rory Gallagher, I brought Larry with me. Looking back, it's hard to deny that my daily drinking and regular cocaine use had something to do with my bad decisions; what happens when your lifestyle instead of your work becomes your priority.

And then it seemed, as if in a freefall, the bottom began to fall out not only of my career but my life as well. Columbia dropped me, Geraldine divorced me, and the IRS wanted to get paid. I was in a state of shock, all this hitting me at once, and decided to leave my management abruptly, thinking I could do it on my own with maybe a vague plan of moving to Paris someday ...

HERE'S THE THING, IF YOU'RE A BAND YOU CAN BREAK UP, GET back together, replace members when they quit or even die, change style ... just about anything you want as long as the name stays the same. There was a time when two *Temptations*, the iconic *Motown* singing group, were touring simultaneously across the US. It's kind of like that recent regretful Supreme Court decision that declared corporations are, in fact, people. Really? Try inviting a corporation over for dinner. Actually, it's the same with rock bands, which are artificially created entities, often false brotherhoods, whose names are often found by musicians thumbing through dictionaries (*Grateful Dead*) or from a phrase in a novel (*Steely Dan*). Or copying other band's names; I mean, why do you think the *Beatles* called themselves that? Because they admired Buddy Holly's band The *Crickets* and went for a similar insect motif. Or as is the case of *The Rolling Stones*, taking the name from a title by one of their idols, Muddy Waters. Should I have called myself *The Gatsby's, The Daisy lovers* or even more obscurely, *The Green Lights at the End of the Dock?* With a band, its often true that the whole is greater than the sum of its parts and if you're a member of a band you have the luxury of referring to that band in the third person or using the royal *we*. Paul McCartney can say, *When the Beatles first walked into a recording studio* **we** *knew we would become the greatest band in the history of recorded music* (he didn't really say that, of course) but if I was to say, *When Elliott Murphy walked into The Record Plant in 1973* ... at this point the journalists, interrupts. *But you are Elliott Murphy?*

So here we get the gist of the problem when you're a solo act like me, a lonely troubadour, a one-man show, the stressed-out wizard pulling the levers behind the curtain in *The Land of Oz*, when the sad truth is that you can't *break up* and get back together, you can only *break down*. And that's what I did in 1978, after *Just A Story from America* did not take me to the top. I broke down completely, mind, body and soul, although I didn't know it at the time. Looking back, I think it's fair to say that my album, and my recording contract, got enmeshed in the middle of a three-way power struggle between Bruce Lundvall head of *Columbia Records*, Walter Yetnikoff, CEO of parent group *CBS Records*, and my managers *Leber-Krebs*. I went out with a whimper and not a bang, when within a year after the album's release, I had a very depressing meeting with Bruce Lundvall at *Black Rock*[7] with my manager Steve Leber and Bruce explained how sorry he was, but they were dropping a lot of acts and I was one of them so don't take it personally. That didn't make me feel better.

My management, Steve Leber and David Krebs, to their credit, tried to re-kindle the interest of Clive Davis, whose label *Arista Records* was now successful. Clive agreed to an in person audition up at his office in the *Arista* building on 57th Street; I was to bring my guitar and sing a few new songs while sitting directly in front of him. A very nerve-racking audition to be sure and to keep it light, I began with *It's Up to You,* a song about my divorce but whose title was certainly very relevant to this very meeting. Clive listened, was very respectful, and greatly complimented me on my songwriting, saying I was as good as anything that was once on FM radio, even compared me to the great Paul Simon, but that times had changed. And he passed.

Clive was right. The music scene in the U.S. had changed drastically in just a few years. *Punk* and *New Wave* defined the zeitgeist and bands such as *The Ramones* and *Talking Heads* had captured the attention of the music press. The UK, no longer exporting blues and rock bands, now specialized in pure pop entities such as the synthesizer sounds of *Human League* and bare-footed singer *Boy George*. Not only did the punks repudiate singer-songwriters such as myself, it seems they also wanted little to do with my former drug of choice, cocaine, preferring the more *authentic* heroin, which hardly fits into the *recreational* drug category. The punk era and its junkie mystique held no allure for me then or now. I talked with Sid Vicious while standing at the bar of the *Mudd Club* and he literally did not say one coherent sentence. He didn't last long...

I remember being in a dressing room at *Max's Kansas City* with Johnny Thunders, ex-New York Dolls guitarist, junkie fashion icon and charismatic *loser*, who was embarking on a solo career in spite of being an unrepentant heroin addict. I knew Johnny from when he played lead guitar with *The New York Dolls,* and there was something sensitive and tender about him in spite of the way he hid behind his *junkie with street smarts* persona. Anyway, around this time, he'd finally managed to record an impressive solo album, *So Alone,* including the memorable track, *You Can't Put Your Arms Around A Memory,* and it looked like Johnny was going to break through to some kind of commercial success in spite of himself. When he split from that *Max's* dressing room for a few minutes, I found myself with four or five of his *closest* friends. Naïvely, I started lecturing them on how this new album of his was Johnny's big opportunity, how they should help him clean up and make sure he didn't blow it. All those in the room emphatically agreed, of course, coming together as one in a compassionate chorus, *We gotta help Johnny!* Soon after, I left that dressing room myself, probably looking for cocaine, and when I returned after Johnny had come back with the *goods,* I swear, everyone in that cramped ugly space had a needle in their arm. There was blood on the walls and bouquets of syringes propping out of bloody glasses of water. It was like *Night of the living dead* had come to town.

In 1977, around the time the now legendary punk and new wave era, largely centered around *CBGB's* in New York, was capturing the media's attention, *Rolling Stone* magazine, which has always possessed an uncanny ability of being at the right place at the right time, moved to New York from San Francisco where the Summer of Love was now a distant memory. Publisher Jann Wenner, thinking I was the quintessential rock-star man about town of the time, asked me to write a piece about the city's hot spots. *Rolling Stone* hired a stretch limo and photographer Lynn Goldsmith accompanied me on a voyage from Midtown to the Bowery, illustrating my story with her fine photos. Together we went to *Manny's Music Store* on West 47th Street where my father had bought me my first electric guitar[8] fifteen years before, then on down to the Village's *The Other End* where I had showcased my album *Aquashow,* and over to the Bowery where *CBGB's* was to the punks what Nashville's *Grand Old Opera* was to country music albeit with a lot more piss on the bathroom floors, and even outside the fearsome CBS *Darth Vader* like headquarters, aka *Black Rock* on 6th Avenue, where my record label *Columbia* occupied many floors. I wrote some wise ass remark about their *expense accounts* department which I thought was witty. *Columbia* didn't, and I imagine this piece killed whatever dwindling support I still had at the label. When Lynn and I arrived at CBGB's one night and I popped out of that stretch limo in a white Yves St. Laurent suit and pink silk tie, recently acquired in Paris on a promo visit for my single *Anastasia,* some punk militant came tearing out of the door, heading right at me. *Get out of here!* He screamed in my face. *We don't need your limos down here!* But he was wrong because in the months to come many other limos followed when the major labels were all sniffing around CBGB's, caught up in a signing frenzy and grabbing acts like *The Ramones, Blondie, Patti Smith* and *Talking Heads*. My article, *Elliott Murphy's Big City Beat* came out in *Rolling Stone's* first New York based edition and soon after I did an interview for *Punk Magazine,* wherein I asked *Can you tell me where's the love in Punk? Because I can't find it*. That interview, veering way too far from the *party line,* was never published.

Chapter Ten

LOST IN THE WILDERNESS

Elliott Murphy with James Dean T-Shirt 1980

Just A Story from America

I'm not sure how it happened but I became a semi-regular at *Studio 54*, the *mother of all discos*, where I began a brief affair with D.D. Ryan, a former Harper's Bazaar editor and socialite who had married into one of New York's richest families. D.D. was older than me but so smart and funny and sophisticated and, like me, *enjoyed* a drink, that I couldn't resist her charms. At this time, I was like a spurned lover, rejecting the world of rock 'n roll, with my photo on the cover of *Women's Wear Daily* while dancing at Studio 54 with another lost love, *Comanche* Indian Carol Shaffer, who would inspire me to write my heartbroken ballad *Texas*. I remember being introduced to Jack Nicholson in the dingy basement VIP room of *Studio 54* after D.D. introduced us, and figuring if Jack was hanging out there, then it must be OK for me to do the same. When Jack said *Hello Elliott* in that laconic voice with his demonic yet irresistible grin, I felt like I was in *The Shining*, surrounded by ghosts, which in a way, I was.

One night after *Studio*, D.D. brought a gang of us all back to her swanky duplex off Sutton Place for more drinks and breakfast. Two baby-grand pianos, dove-tailed next to each other, were covered with silver Tiffany framed photos of the legions of *fabulous* people D.D. knew and loved, including Liza Minnelli who was actually there with us that night, just as vivacious and charming as you'd expect her to be. Being with Liza was like being on the set of *Cabaret*;[1] an absolutely luminous show biz veneer as if a spotlight had suddenly focused on her smile. She also had that inexplicable movie star magnetism that made you adore her at first sight, which I did, and when she felt like singing, DD suggested I accompany her, being the only musician there that night. We both sat down on the piano bench, and of course, Liza wanted to sing Broadway show tunes of which I knew none. I tried to get her to try singing well known Dylan songs, of which *she* didn't know any. Finally, in a classy gesture that allowed both of us to save face, she gently placed her hands upon mine as they rested on that piano keyboard, keeping them still while she sang a few numbers totally *A cappella*. But still I would have loved to hear her sing *Like A Rolling Stone*:

Ahh you've gone to the finest schools, alright Miss Lonely - But you know you only used to get juiced in it ...

And Liza, if you're listening, let's do it again sometime but this time let's rehearse!

Becoming a part of that privileged *Studio* crowd, if ever so briefly, I came in contact with other fascinating characters through D.D. as well; the suave designer Halston, *Studio 54* owner Steve Rubell who sat on his lap, and most notably, the photographer Peter Beard, the most fearless and enigmatic man I ever knew. Beautiful women literally flocked to Peter like moths to a flame and he would sometimes invite a handful of gorgeous models to join us for dinner at *Elaine's*, an Upper East Side watering hole for the *jet-set* (an extinct *tribe* which has evolved, Darwinian like, into the *private jet-set*), and each of these stunning creatures would be under the impression that *she* was the *one*, she was Peter's date for the evening and the others were mere set decorations. The best part was recording the background music for Peter's *End of the Game* photo exhibit at the *International Center of Photography*, then located across from the *Metropolitan Museum*, on 5th Avenue. We incorporated the eerie sounds of blue whales and with the help of Ernie Brooks and my vivacious backing vocalist Jennifer Torres, did a slowed-down version of Buddy Holly's *Not Fade,* apropos to an exhibit that contained multiple images of dead African elephants, who died of constipation when forced to eat trees as humans encroached further and further on their territory. And there was an original song, *Hesitation and Perfume*, again inspired by *Johnson and Johnson* heiress, Libet Johnson. Peter seemed to know everybody you wanted to know in New York at that time, from Mick Jagger to the Kennedy clan. I remember sharing a dessert with Caroline Kennedy, who seemed mature and focused and always quick to *cut to the chase*, all very *Kennedyesque* qualities. I also shook

Just A Story from America

hands with her mother, Jacqueline Kennedy Onassis, when we ran into her on Madison Avenue walking her dog and smoking, and I remember her distinct accent, something between a *preppie* and East Hampton, Long Island where she grew up; slim and stylish, still with her beautifully coiffed quintessential *bouffant*. There was also the brilliant Democratic politician Allard Lowenstein, a leader of the anti-war movement in congress who would be murdered in his office by a mentally ill gunman just a few years later.

The year of *End of the Game* was Peter's moment, it seemed like he was at the epicenter of everything that happened in the city, and everybody who was important and beautiful wanted to know him. Carole Bouquet, then a young French actress breezed through town, hung out at *Studio 54* with Peter and charmed us all before disappearing back to Paris where she went on to achieve enormous international film success, even appearing as a *James Bond* girl in 1981's *For Your Eyes Only*. Years later, when I left Lou Reed at the *Plaza Athénée Hotel*, I ran into Carole right outside on Avenue Montaigne and she remembered me, gave me her phone number and said to give her a call. And fool that I am, I lost her number! Damn!

While setting up the music playback at the *International Center of Photography* for Peter's *End of the Game* photo exhibition, I worked briefly with Cornell Capra, the younger brother of famed war photographer Robert Capra, who died in Vietnam. Cornell, a photographer himself, was director of the ICP and also, while there, I fell deeply in love with a stunning beautiful Texan, part Comanche Indian, Carol Shaffer. Carol was the best thing that had happened to me since my double divorce from both Geraldine and *Columbia Records*. During our brief affair, I followed her down to Mexico and drove through the night from Houston to Nuevo Laredo where impoverished Mexican kids sold *Chiclets* by the piece, and on to Matamoros, an oil town on the gulf. Carol was only woman I ever dated who owned a pistol, but then again, she was from Texas. When we were photographed dancing together in *Studio 54* and that shot appeared on the front page of *Women's Wear Daily*, I remember thinking it was not a very rock 'n roll image, even if Mick Jagger threw a birthday party for his then wife Bianca in the same elitist joint, where she entered onto the dance floor on a white stallion. I'm not sure what all that was about, if it was meaningful or part of my spiritual journey but I'm glad I did it, because between *Studio 54, The Mudd Club* and *Elaine's,* I was there at the epicenter of an iconic era in New York City's pop history.

But financially, I couldn't keep up with the crowd that ran with Peter Beard; I had no trust fund keeping me afloat and my *American Express* bill was now into five digits. D.D. Ryan offered to loan me money but that wasn't my style. So, I said goodbye to *Elaine's* and all that, licked my wounds, leased a tan *Mercedes Benz*, rented a cozy beach house for a while where I was up close and personal with Vicky, a 17-year-old local out in Amagansett. On snowy winter nights, I would drive into the city, pick up Ernie Brooks, and get my foolish kicks spinning that car in circles on the icy roads. We hung out mostly at the *Mudd Club*, which was like a smart version of *CBGB's* where one memorable night I stole kisses from film star Patti D'Arbanville, who not only inspired the Cat Stevens' hit *Lady D'Arbanville,* but was also, a world class kisser. I also dated Michael Jackson's charismatic star publicist Susan Blond who re-introduced me to Andy Warhol. On the music side, I retreated into the bottom rungs of the only world I knew, that of the rock clubs, and with a power trio of Ernie, Tony Machine and myself, began playing as many shows as I could; often driving to Boston, or Canada, or even all the way out to Cleveland, just for one-nighters. When I left my management company, I thought I could do it all on my own, and soon was forced to move out of my swanky apartment on East 72nd Street and put just about everything I couldn't carry with me into storage while me and my guitars moved into my mother's apartment, sleeping on a cot in her dining room. I had next to nothing.

After confiding in me that she was suffering from cancer, Carol and I broke up, breaking my heart in so many pieces I didn't know where to start looking to pick them up. Shortly after that, I was drinking at the *Lone Star* Café, licking my wounds, when I was presented to legendary songwriter Doc Pomus, sitting in a wheelchair, and who had not only written the Drifters' *Save the last dance for me*, but also Elvis Presley's hit *Marie's the name of his latest flame*. I think it must have been Larry "Ratso" Sloman, man about town and editor of *High Times* magazine who introduced us. To be honest, I don't remember whose show we were all there for, maybe Townes Van Zandt, maybe Rick Danko, both tragic figures, both long gone now as well, as is Doc himself. *The Rock 'n Roll Hall of Fame* should construct a *memorial wall*, something like the *Vietnam War Memorial* in Washington DC, where names of all the dead and missing rock musicians will be inscribed for eternity although I hope my name will not be up there for a very, very long time. If I haven't said it already I'll say it again, success in the music business is measured by survival. And I survived.

I played the *The Lone Star* a dozen times in the late seventies and early eighties, although that club and my music was a strange fit because for all intents and purposes, that rowdy club was really a Texas beer hall moved up north with a giant, and I do mean *giant*, fluorescent green Iguana sculpture sitting on the roof of the building. Most of the acts appearing there were either from Texas or down that way, but it was also home to many visiting blues legends such as John Lee Hooker, who I shared a bill with, and who inspired me to write my homage to the men and women who laid the groundwork for rock 'n roll, *Blues Responsibility:*

John Lee Hooker sits on stage - Patent leather shoes - Never misses a beat
Two white girls - Frizzy hair light cigarettes - Endless boogie - Boom, boom, boom - One two...

Owner Mort Cooperman and I got along well and thanks to Carol's *cowgirl couture* influence, I was sporting lizard *Lucchese* cowboy boots, bought down at *Cutter Bill's* in Houston with her, fitting in with the current urban cowboy look, although I've yet to ride a mechanized bull. I was proud to be standing on the same stage as such great artists as Willie Nelson and Roy Orbison. I think it was Duke Ellington who was said there are only two kinds of music, *good and bad*! Or to be even more succinct, in the words of Townes Van Zandt, *There's only two kinds of music: the blues and zippety doo-dah*. Anyway, that night at the Lone Star, I came right out and asked Doc Pomus what was his secret to writing a hit song and he replied it was simple, you just got to get your heart broken first and then write a song about it. *And if you want to write a follow-up?* I asked. *Just go out there and get your heart broken again*, said Doc. It made sense. Carol had broken my heart and as I sat in that bar around closing time, I began to jot down the words to *Last Call* on a cocktail napkin, a ballad which appeared on my 1982 album *Party Girls and Broken Poets* and broken-hearted (I imagine) fans still call out for it in concert. It would be perfect for Kenny Rogers, by the way.

In December 1978, I was invited to come to Japan for a two-week tour, bringing Ernie Brooks, my *still* faithful bassist, and my brother Matthew, now my manager, along with me. Arriving at a crowded press conference the first morning in our Tokyo hotel, I was bowled over by the feverish music media attention the tour was generating among the Japanese press. They asked me what I called the type of music I would play on this tour and I looked at Ernie and thought for a minute ... *Punk Folk*, I finally replied. There was dead silence among the assembled journalists as a mad scribbling of pens in notebooks ensued; surely these collected writers, rock specialists all, had never heard of such a kind of music before but then again, *punk* and *new wave* had only recently entered the pop lexicon, so I guess they figured anything was possible. Within a few days, the name of that new and exciting genre, *Punk Folk*, was born, splicing Pete Seeger's *Where have all the flowers gone* with The Ramone's *I want to be sedated*; splashed on every music rag in the land. I was even more surprised that the Japanese audience seemed to know my song *Drive All Night* before I discovered that a popular Japanese band, *The*

Roosters, had scored a hit with it. Of course, no one back in the US, not my publisher, manager or record company, had bothered to tell me about it. And I was even more astounded when *Sony Records Japan* offered me a contract, saying I would have *carte blanche* to record in their new state-of-the-art digital studios in Tokyo. Perhaps foolishly, Matthew and I politely turned them down; both of us thinking that a bigger deal would be waiting for us in America. But they were not waiting and when I returned home no one seemed to care about my triumphant Japanese tour.

WALKING DOWN 57TH STREET AROUND THIS TIME, I RAN INTO Jann Wenner, the publisher of *Rolling Stone,* whom I had known for years. I met Jann early on when together we were guests on a TV pilot for a rock 'n roll talk show that never made it to the networks. I always liked him; very bright guy with a rock 'n roll heart. He asked what I was doing, and I was honest, saying not much, writing poems, writing short stories, and he enthusiastically said he'd very much like to see both. Not many poems have made it to the pages of *Rolling Stone* but a few of mine have! When Jann read a short story I was working on, *Cold and Electric,* about a guitarist on the skids who's trying to climb back up the rock 'n roll mountain after reaching a peak and then falling back down, his interest in my writing became even more serious. The hero of the story was Marty May, and his predicament was inspired by Scott Fitzgerald's *Pat Hobby Stories,* which were written at a low point in his own career; about a hustling screenwriter trying to survive in Hollywood. Scott died just a few years after publishing many of the *Pat Hobby* stories in *Esquire,* something I was hoping not to do. Jann edited *Cold and Electric* himself, actually using the original *cut and paste* mode of real scissors and glue, before publishing it in the magazine's double 1980 year-end issue. Finally, my name was on the cover of *Rolling Stone!* I was a published author now, my work in a respected magazine, and not so surprisingly, soon after that I got a call from a vice president of the Hollywood film studio, 20*th* *Century Fox*. A meeting was arranged the next week at the *Sherry Netherlands Hotel* and, *hallelujah*, I thought, my ship had finally come in. Ultimately, 20*th Century Fox* decided not to turn the story into a film because after some research, they came to the *erroneous* conclusion that rock 'n roll films don't click with the grand public. I say *erroneous* because I think the *right* one has yet to be made. But ladies and gentlemen, *Marty May* is ready for his closeup.

At the next *Rolling Stone* Christmas party, I had a brief conversation with Hunter S. Thompson who was magnetically charming in a *gonzo* sort of way while we both sat at a table drinking. I have no idea how Hunter knew that F. Scott Fitzgerald was my main man, but he brought his name up right away, telling me that Scott was his favorite author as well. I was dumfounded. *Fear and Loathing in West Egg!*[2] Not discouraged by 20*th* Century Fox rejection, Jann Wenner encouraged me to turn *Cold and Electric* into a full-blown novel and I worked for months up at the *Rolling Stone* office with a sympathetic editor, Patti Romanowski, doing just that. But ultimately, even as powerful a force as *Rolling Stone* was, even they could not find an interested co-publisher; many of them rejecting the book using almost the same line as 20*th Century Fox* had used when rejecting it for a film: *people who like that kind of music don't read books*.

Jann Wenner assured me, in his infinite wisdom, that someday *Marty May*, the main character in *Cold and Electric*, would find a home and eventually, in 2012, the historic French publisher *Gallimard* published the full novel in a fine French translation by Christophe Mercier, now and forever called *Marty May*, on their prestigious *Joelle Losfeld* imprint. *Gallimard* was an appropriate match because I always felt that the alienated character of rock guitarist Marty May, who tells much of his story in the 1*st* person, had something in common with Albert Camus' antihero Meursault, in his novel *The Stranger,* which was also first published by *Gallimard*.

The early 1980's were not only tough on my bank account but

also debilitating on my soul and I often spent pointless afternoons walking through the skyscraper canyons of Manhattan, feeling like a condemned man, drinking beer hidden within a brown paper bag. My life went from the sublime to the ridiculous. I remember sitting in the office of Jimmy Poulis, *JP* we called him, after a show at his west side club TRAX with Willie Deville and John Belushi and *Rolling Stones Records* president Earl McGrath, drinking and snorting coke. I may have been a forgotten man but Belushi, who was at the peak of his career, seemed like a man on a mission to destroy himself fast. He was in much worse shape than myself, while Willie was taking the *slow boat to China*, strung out on heroin, dressed in a shiny suit. Now they are all dead. Only I'm left standing. There must be a reason …

I PLAYED A SHOW IN ASBURY PARK AT *THE FASTLANE* AND BRUCE Springsteen came down to see me; even offering that I could stay at his place, which was nearby, if I didn't want to drive all the way back to New York after the gig. In the years since we had first been introduced by Paul Nelson, I had run into Bruce a few times, once while standing in line for a film on 3rd Avenue, and he was always extremely friendly with not a trace of arrogance even as his popularity was growing exponentially. That night, I let the band hassle with the gear and drove off into the Jersey night, following Bruce in his vintage 1960 *Corvette*. He was living in a spacious old farmhouse, rented, that actually abutted a working farmer's field. Entering the place, I smiled when I saw that his band's gear, and I'm talking the *E-Street band* here, was set up for rehearsal right in the living room, the finest and largest room of the house. *This is how it's supposed to look like,* I thought. The band's equipment was all right there when you walked in the room, from Clarence Clemons's glistening sax resting on a stand to Bruce's own famed *Telecaster*. Bruce cooked up something called *Steakums*, thinly sliced beef paddies that you fried up and put between bread. A south Jersey acquired taste, I presumed, and played me some demos of his newly written songs including the punk influenced *Roulette,* telling me that he'd been listening to the *Sex Pistols* a lot lately and wanted to record something with that same kind of energy. We talked well into the night and Bruce explained that he had always put his music first, never allowing any material comforts or objects to slow him down, living in rented houses such as this where if he bought furniture or anything else for the house he just left it there when he left. He told me that after the *River tour,* he bought himself a black lacquered *Yamaha* baby grand piano and that *Chevrolet Corvette,* black too if I remember correctly, because he couldn't think of anything else he really needed. I knew what he really *needed,* and still needs, was the same thing I was lacking, the healing power that only a live audience can provide; material comforts were only temporary distractions. But Bruce was a wise man, old for his age, and he knew this about himself long before I did about me. It wasn't until I began touring Europe that I really learned my craft, learned to play for my fans, learned to make the road a permanent part of my life, that I understood his motivation, his *raison d'etre.* I've now played over 2500 shows and still counting. Not stopping soon.

Bruce has righteously both celebrated and defended the day-to-day struggle of those living in the blue-collar milieu he grew up around, and in the process of doing that became very rich himself, while I, who was sometimes perceived as chronicling the angst of the privileged class in songs like *Rich Girls* and *Diamonds by the Yard,* was broke. Ironic, eh? There's a lesson to be learned there that I definitely didn't learn early enough. My mother, who wasn't brought up privileged at all, her father being an insurance salesman who commuted to Brooklyn each day, always told me *sell to the masses and you can eat with the classes* and attributed that quote to Henry Ford. Actually, my favorite Ford quote is when many years after the *Ford Model T* had taken the country by storm, he was asked if he thought the public wanted an automobile at the time he introduced it and he replied, *no, what they wanted was faster horses.*

Somewhat like the automobile business, the music business is a *winner take all game* and when the dust clears usually only a few bands or artists are left standing, to keep going on to the next decade, the next musical revolution, be it FM radio or Compact Discs or *iTunes* or *Spotify*, so you better make your mark when you're young and attract fans who will stick to you for life. Right now, I'm sitting here listening to one of my own tracks, *Change Will Come*, written in the late 70's when I was lost in the wilderness, without a record label, thinking my career was over.

It's all right mama, it's all right now, I never really wanted any of it anyhow.

Change Will Come was going to be my re-entry in 1986 when I connected with Jim Ball, an engineer at *The Record Plant*, and he offered to produce some of my new songs at this still great studio that was hanging in there as New York rents skyrocketed and west coast recording studios took over. The sessions went smoothly, although to support myself I was working in an uptown law firm during the day as a legal secretary and recording at night often until dawn left me exhausted. But in spite of that, Jim and I we were so sure, so *damn sure*, that this was it, that surely some major label would have to pick this album up. But finally, after a few false starts, nothing happened, I wasn't going to be let back *into the club* after all and the album was released in Europe where it did well for an independent album from an independent artist, which is what I am now and have been for the last thirty-five years.

I was often taking my meals at *Cottonwood*, a Tex-Mex restaurant on Bleecker Street. Even ate there with Bruce Springsteen one time when the waitress did a double take and then shook her head and decided *no this can't possibly be him* and left us alone. *Cottonwood* had fine *chicken fried steak* and *corn bread* and good singers performing on its small stage. There was this one thin girl with a big guitar who stood out from the others, the plaintive cry in her voice forcing customers look up from their *enchiladas* and pay attention. A beautiful girl with beautiful songs and fine voice, named Shawn Colvin. I got to know her a bit, said she was from North Dakota, I always remember that because she was the only person I ever met from that far off state. Anyway, when it was time for some backing vocals on *Change Will Come* I called Shawn in the middle of the night and she agreed to hop in a cab and come up to the *Record Plant* to sing. We had no budget to speak of, so Jim Ball paid her $50 out of his own pocket plus cab fare – not even sure if we covered the cab. Shawn sang marvelously on three songs, especially *Chain of Pain*, and within a few years had her own deal on a major label and then an enormous and well-deserved nationwide hit with *Sunny Came Home* in 1987.

Can I say that I discovered Shawn Colvin before anyone else? Not really, because true talent shines through *whatever* as Shawn had shone through when just her presence on that small stage forced customers put down their *Tequilas* and *ribs* at Cottonwood and listen up. Another great singer, Blondie Chaplin of *Beach Boys* fame[3], sang on *Change Will Come* as well. Blondie was hanging out with my pal David Johansen, ex-*New York Dolls* front man who had a few solo albums out under his own name and finally a hit, *Hot, hot, hot* under his party animal personae, *Buster Poindexter*. David and I often tried to write some songs together and came up with one that made it on to his *Here Comes the Night* solo album, *Havin' So Much Fun*, about trying to have a good time after a break-up which is kind of what I was doing when I lived on Gramercy Park South and David lived on 16th Street. *Tramps, our clubhouse* as David use to call it, was on 15th Street and my drummer Tony Machine lived on 17th Street. The real music star of the neighborhood was keyboardist Paul Shaffer, who led the *Saturday Night Live* band and later went on be musical director on *The David Letterman* show. Paul lived in the *Gramercy Park Hotel*, right across the park from my own apartment building and we'd often run into each other. Once, when I was late to some appointment, rushing as usual, and ran into Paul he stopped and said,

Elliott Murphy, always in a hurry, always in shades, and I was both. It was the kind of line he became famous for on the Letterman show.

When Chrissie Hynde of *The Pretenders* turned up at David Johansen's apartment one afternoon to give a helping hand at co-writing some songs, I happened to be there, and I suggested we try to write something called *And God Created Women*, inspired by the Roger Vadim film with Brigitte Bardot. We tried a few things, threw some lines and melodies around, but no one was really into it except me. Pity!

∼

Chapter Eleven

TAKING THE SILENCE

Singer David Johansen, star publicist Susan Blond and Elliott Murphy at Studio 54

*I*n the language of the Native Americans, who inhabited the Great Lakes region, the word *Milwaukee* means *a gathering place by the water* and it was the city that changed my life for just that reason. Jerry Harrison, a Milwaukee native, had been my keyboard player for much of *Night Lights* and the tour that preceded it and his piano parts on *Diamonds by The Yard,* were stunning and precise. Like his fellow ex-*Modern Lover* Ernie Brooks, Jerry was a Harvard graduate with a rock 'n roll heart. I still can't justify why I fired Jerry Harrison (as well as Andy Paley) from the band; it was more a case of moving on to something else rather than asking them to leave. It was probably a mistake, one of many I might add, but Jerry wanted to push the band in a more R&B direction; he loved James Brown as much as I loved Bob Dylan, probably even more, and there was pressure from my management, particularly my day-to-day guy, Kevin McShane, to put together a band that was, how should I say, less *Harvard*. I kept Ernie Brooks on bass though, because he was a poet at heart and he loved Robert Lowell[1] even more then James Brown or Bob Dylan.

I think Jerry toyed with the idea of going back to Harvard and getting his *master's* degree in architecture but through some *Deus ex machina*, after a short interlude, he joined the band he was born for, *The Talking Heads*; a few years later my own brother became their tour manager which was ironic, to say that least, while I was in residence at *Tramps*, the Irish cum Blues bar on East 15th Street, where the bartender was a coke dealer, where the *Guinness Stout* flowed freely, where I hit my bottom. But Jerry didn't hold a grudge, always a big-hearted guy, and besides, being thrown out of my band was the best thing that ever happened to him when you consider where he landed. With the *Talking Heads* taking time off, Jerry would come down to *Tramps* to take in my show and hang out with Ernie, who was still playing bass with me. I had sunken pretty low by that point, and I like to think Jerry had taken pity on me, at least enough to suggest we go out to his hometown *Milwaukee* to record some music together. He had some interesting ideas about producing *Out for The Killing* and *Texas,* two new songs and part of my regular *Tramps* repertoire, at DV Studios, located in Shorewitch, the Milwaukee suburb where he grew up.

I booked a flight that left on a Sunday evening; Jerry was already in Milwaukee and would meet me at the airport, with recording beginning bright and early on Monday. That I have noted the days of the week is not trivial because I knew that Saturday was a dangerous party night, if I wasn't out playing, and yet on Monday I had to be in shape to begin what could be my biggest career lucky break in years. I distinctly remember that Saturday evening, feeling anxious in my closet size flat on Gramercy Park, so afraid if I went out that night I would go off on a binge, miss the flight and blow it all. I debated with myself until midnight before deciding I better go down to *Tramps* and have a few beers just to calm my nerves. Well, as you might guess, come Sunday morning, I was back in my apartment checking my pulse which was dangerously hovering around one-fifty; hadn't slept all night, and my cocaine vial was empty. I was chugging vodka, dropping *Valium* and I was praying, *God, get me through this and I'll never do it again.* This fix, as horrible as it might appear, was nothing new for me. During the ten years before, I had been in the same woeful shape on more times than I could count; coming down from booze and drugs, scared I was overdosing, and praying to some *God*, who I really had no relation with whatsoever, for deliverance from my misery. The only song that gave me comfort was Kris Kristofferson's *Sunday Morning Coming Down*. At least I wasn't alone…

And in fact, I *wasn't* alone because something happened, different then all those other times, and a voice spoke to me, not a supernatural voice, not any kind of a mystical presence or metaphysical trip, but a voice deep within myself, almost like the thoughts of my forgotten *core*, struggling to survive. And this is what that voice told me: *Elliott, you can forget the prayers to this God of your childhood, forget the bargaining, because this is what you do, the cocaine and the booze and all that goes with it, and this is what you'll continue to do until something bad happens. And if you accept this about yourself than everything will be ok.* And then I fell asleep, which as anyone with any experience with cocaine knows, is a miracle in itself. That evening I caught the flight, Jerry picked me up at the airport in his Pontiac Lemans convertible and my new life was about to begin.

In Milwaukee, we went to dinner at *The Coffee Trader,* a hip restaurant that Jerry liked to hang out at, located in a complex of stylish ground floor boutiques among which was a chic fitness center called *Stretch*. We sat down to dinner and the owner came over to say hello to Jerry, the local rock celebrity, bringing with him Rita, the cute red-haired woman who owned and ran *Stretch*. I immediately was attracted to her in a way I wasn't usually attracted to women; something very positive about her was pulling me into her orbit. I don't remember how fast it happened, if I got her number that night or returned to take classes at her fitness studio first, but soon we were driving around Milwaukee in her white two-seater *Mercedes* convertible. I couldn't believe my luck, until without prompting, she told me she didn't drink alcohol, hadn't had a drink in over two years, and how her recovery had saved her life. I was impressed the more I learned about Rita; hers was a moving story, a very traumatic childhood, a pursuant struggle to find her way and ultimate redemption. And what was my response? I said I wish I had a drinking problem, but my problem was cocaine. I could handle alcohol fine, I thought.

"When do you use coke?" she asked.

"Well, when I'm out – I start drinking and, you know, one thing leads to another," I replied innocently enough.

I imagine, right about then, Rita must have wanted to break out laughing. But she didn't. Instead, on our next date, she brought along a questionnaire she thought might interest me, which contained a series of questions that, depending on your response, would indicate if you had a problem with alcohol or not. Not surprisingly, I answered positive to nearly every question but one: *Do you drink in the morning?* No, I didn't drink alcohol in the morning. I was off the hook.

"What time do you wake up?" asked Rita.

"Around three in the afternoon," I said.

This brought, if not barrels of laughter, at least a knowing smirk to Rita's face. She asked if I wanted to go with her to a gathering of people who had stopped drinking and taking drugs. I thought of the meaning of *Milwaukee*, a gathering by the lake, and for some unknown reason, maybe that *core* voice again, I reluctantly agreed. Honestly, what I was interested in was Rita, not stopping drinking, but I went along with her a few evenings later with the promise that I wouldn't have to say one word to anyone for the hour that I was there. The meeting was held in a suburban church basement, reminding me of the Garden City *Community Church*, where I went to Sunday school as a *kid*, and it seemed that just moments after I sat in my chair, the woman who was leading this *gathering*, asked if there was *anybody* here for the first time who might want to introduce themselves ... and pointed directly to me. I must have given severe *dagger eyes* to Rita as I grudgingly raised my hand. *I'm Elliott ... and I'm here checking this meeting out. I don't know if I have a problem with alcohol but ...* Before I could even finish my sentence and add more feeble efforts at denial, I got a huge round of applause from the assembled *gathering*. What I didn't realize, and Rita was quick to point out, was that there was actually someone sitting behind me, another newcomer who had raised their hand. From that day on I guess I owned my seat.

Half-way through the meeting we broke into small groups, sitting around folding tables, and I had a sinking feeling when I was stuck with the squarest group of people I ever did a real *sit-down* with; I mean these folks didn't know *Chuck Berry* from *The Raspberrys*; they were insurance agents, teachers, all kinds of *normal people* but not one musician, no hipsters at all. We went around that table and shared our stories. I listened and then I talked and then I listened some more, and something miraculous happened because when I stood up at that end of the meeting, I felt like this group of people, who had never listened to any of my music, really knew who I was and what my fears were, where my demons lived. And I haven't had a drink or a drug since that day, thirty-three years and counting. If you want to know what a miracle looked like in the 20th Century, it happened at that meeting with those people that night.

I never went to a rehab, no snazzy *Betty Ford* clinic for me, and just started counting days without a drink as my life started to change for the better right away. We finished recording *Milwaukee* with the help of Olympic swimming coach John Collins, who provided some financial support, and I returned to New York ready to show the world the new Elliott Murphy ready to rock.

Chapter Twelve

THE REVENANT

Elliott Murphy performing solo in Sweden 1981

Just A Story from America

In 1979 I had played my first show in Paris at *Le Palace* on rue Montmartre, just a few blocks from where I now live. I was still with ICM, a major booking agency and had an agent there named Ron Zeeluns who was responsible for me whatever that meant. I'm not quite sure how this chic French disco, kind of the *Studio 54* of Paris, tracked me down to Ron but they did and said they wanted to book me for a show with my band. Ron drew up the necessary contracts and we went to Paris, my first time singing and playing guitar in Europe since my 1971 epiphany, when I was busking on the streets. I brought Ernie Brooks on bass and Tony Machine on drums, a power trio of sorts; expecting *Le Palace* to be a small club with maybe a couple of hundred people. But that night, 23rd April 1979, *Le Palace* was full, over a thousand fans, and I did six encores. When I finally left the stage I heard that *Last Tango in Paris* star Maria Schneider was waiting to say hello backstage. Still, in spite of that triumph, and the tours that followed which always required expensive trans-continental flights for me and my band, five years later I was still struggling to stay afloat with just my music and I was working a day job in a law firm in New York City as a legal secretary. I think in my head I had never let go of the desire to *make it* in America; often playing for peanuts while driving five hours back and forth from New York to Boston in the wee hours after a gig to save on hotels. Positive reviews of both my shows and albums continued to pour in but as much as me and my brother tried, we couldn't get another US major record label interested. When *Rolling Stone* reviewed my first indie release, the six song EP *Affairs*, the reviewer even mentioned that he hoped I would find the means to fully produce my albums in the future. But I never found another major label deal in America and eventually I stopped beating my head against the brick wall of the US music business and moved to Paris for good in 1989 where things happened fast. Follow your passions and you just might find yourself *living the dream*.

This *career-affirming* reception I had received at *Le Palace* did not come as a total surprise as *Anastasia,* the French single from my last album, had done quite well there. But I knew less about my earlier albums history there: that *Aquashow* had been released two times, that *Night Lights* had gotten rave reviews, that an interview with French novelist, Pascal Garnier, when I played *The Boarding House* in San Francisco in 1976 had begun to establish my reputation as a live performer, *un bete sur le scene,* as they French sometimes call me. I didn't know any of this and my perception of my career was warped. I had been looking at the top ten of the *Billboard* charts and wondering why my albums were in the bottom 200. My view had been jaundiced by the insatiable expectations of the music business. I thought my career was over, but really it was only just beginning. Psychologists say that children need love and adults need acknowledgement and that night at *Le Palace* I received both in spades.

Soon, other European countries joined France in welcoming me and I began touring extensively in Italy, Belgium, Holland and Sweden. When I finally played a show in Spain in 1983 it was as if I was the first rock singer-songwriter to make an impact in that once isolated country. Franco had only died in 1975 so I *was* among the first rock acts to tour the new *liberated* Spain. In Madrid, I appeared on an important nationwide TV show, *La Edad de Oro* [Golden Age], performing three songs with my band. Journalist were asking for my next album and after a bit of research, I discovered that you could *license* a finished album to independent labels all over Europe and their small advances, when added up, might cover the cost of recording. My first release was a mini-EP called *Affairs* with six songs. In 1980, I started a label *Courtisane Records* with my brother Matthew and my muse, the beautiful free-spirit Cathleen Smith who would grace the covers of three of my albums in provocative poses.

I met Cathy through my drummer Tony Machine, who was working as a doorman in her building. He told me of this beautiful girl from Georgia, who wore high heels, seamed stockings and *Chanel* suits almost every day, who was a fan of mine, having caught my opening set for *Electric Light Orchestra* at the Omni Arena in Atlanta when she was fifteen years old. We bonded, and Cathy was the preemptive step in getting my life together for a while. I found a small studio on *Gramercy* Park with no light and hardly room for more then two people but it was mine and I could move out of my mother's dining room. Cathy and I shared some unforgettable adventures together; she took me to Berlin when the wall was still up, where we crossed *Checkpoint Charlie* and found East Berlin grey and depressing with nothing to buy; we rode in gondolas in Venice and shopped in Florence; and had a wild weekend in New Orleans French Quarter where I drank *Pimms Cup* and ate *jumbalaya* at the *Napoleon Bar* and learned about the origins of jazz at *Preservation Hall*. When a local *Tramps* habituee wanted to celebrate his birthday, Cathy organized a genuine strip-tease with a few of her friends. I'm sure this lucky fellow has yet to have another birthday like that.

Cathy liked doing things *her own way* when the powers that be stood in the way and she encouraged Matthew and I to begin our own record company and stop waiting on some A&R man's whims. We started *Courtisane Records* and pressed thousands of *Affairs* vinyl LPs at a Broadway sweat shop staffed by hard working Polish women immigrants. When I went to visit, I finally saw how a record is actually made, how a *stamping* machine performs *alchemy* by transforming a glob of vinyl into a beautifully grooved work of art as these ladies nonchalantly slipped the labels in-between the hazardous hot presses of the machine. We were selling well, all over America and in Europe too, and I learned more about the actual business of selling music by starting that label then when I was signed to Polydor, RCA or Columbia. There was a string of record stores in NYC called *Crazy Eddie* and the manager of one was a big fan. Thanks to him, they were selling hundreds of *Affairs* and it was a challenge just to keep up with the orders. Matthew was out on tour with Robert Gordon and *Talking Heads,* so there were times when it was I who was minding the *Courtisane* office. One afternoon a call came in, *Crazy Eddie* needed a box of twenty-five *Affairs* right away, so I grabbed one and headed downtown in a taxi. Once inside, I asked the first person I saw where the manager was, and he pointed to the back. When the guy saw me he almost dropped whatever was in his hands to the floor.

"You ordered the Elliott Murphy records?" I asked.

"You're Elliott Murphy?" he said.

"That's right," I answered.

"And you deliver the records yourself?"

"Well," I answered semi-seriously, "...*after what I've been through in the music business, now I want total control.*"

He nodded his head in sympathy.

I learned how to record an album on a slim budget, to get it right the first time, to find second tier studios and bring the best out of them and most importantly, to keep my band working so we'd be tight when we got in the recording studio. I played gigs at *Max's Kansas City* and even *CBGB's* even though it was a dump and owner Hilly Krystal never gave me the time of day. Most of all, I continued to play at *Tramps*, an Irish Blues bar on 15th Street. Once I moved out of my mother's dining room into that very small studio on Gramercy Park, I felt my life was starting to begin again. I was even able to cut out the cocaine for long periods of time, but it kept calling me back until that fateful trip to Milwaukee when I became deaf to its deadly siren's call. I continued to write for *Rolling Stone*, *Spin* and magazines in Europe and Japan; doing interviews with Tom Waits and Keith Richards and Peter Buck from *REM* and most importantly, whatever my psychic condition, I always wrote songs, played shows, put out records. Some critics have put down my albums from the eighties, criticizing the modest production, but they miss the point because even though I didn't have the budget for the production these albums deserved, I *did* have the songs and many of those songs are still in my repertoire today.

I'm in the *museum era* of my career now; and that entails a necessity to ensure my legacy however I can, to prove that my *love was not in vain* to paraphrase blues *tragedian* Robert Johnson. I don't want to go down as an *also-ran*, one of the many *New-Dylan's*, which was a cheap shot to begin with. I mean Bob was only 35 when critics started referring to myself, Bruce Springsteen, Louden Wainwright, John Prine and a host of other *talented* new-comers as just that. Was Jean-Michel Basquiat pinned with the label the *New Picasso?* I met Jean-Michel in 1981 while shooting the film *Downtown 81* directed by *Interview* columnist Glenn O'Brien and Jean-Michel straightaway did his best to not ingratiate himself to me when I introduced myself. That exact conversation, which took place in the backseat of a white stretch limousine, went almost verbatim like this:

Me: "Hi Jean-Michel, I'm Elliott Murphy, how you doing?"

Jean-Michel (looking away): "I hear you're a has-been."

That pissed me off so much that I refused to buy any of the drawings he was selling for a hundred bucks each, I imagine to buy dope. The lesson here is never let your wounded pride get in the way of a good investment. The movie itself, released years later as *Downtown 81*, also featured the wonderful and ageless Debbie Harry of *Blondie*, who, or so I hear, had the good sense to buy a few of Jean-Michel's drawings. In the film, I was playing the part of a rock star and Glenn had sent the Limo to pick me up both as a favor and to put me in character so to speak. I think Jean-Michel didn't like that he had to take the subway to the set while I rode in style, so when he sat in the back seat with me he already had a serious resentment going. Suffice it to say, the *has-been* is still *right-here* while Jean-Michel Basquiat is forever a *no-more*, dead at the unlucky age of 27 of the deadly triple combination of drugs, instant fame and a shitty attitude.

Painters? I envy them because they only have to sell a painting to one buyer at a time while I've got to sell a song a thousand times over if I want to keep in business. I did once have the honor of hanging out for an evening with *the* grand abstract expressionist Willem de Kooning, out on Long Island at his house in Springs and he was very cool and humble indeed. At the time, I was dating Tina Cato, a close friend of Willem's daughter Lisa, whose father was the famed album designer Bob Cato; don't know if that job description even exists anymore. Anyway, the three of us went to Willem de Kooning's modest ranch house, white with red trim, one night to watch the mini-series *Roots*[1] on TV. Willem was still dressed in white overalls splattered with paint, and he resembled what I imagined to be a modern Vincent Van Gogh, speaking with a soft Dutch accent albeit with both ears intact. The walls to his living room were lined with rows of illuminated glass cabinets full of pre-Columbian art, little figurines either pregnant or with big dicks half their size. Lisa, Tina and I sat caddy corner from Willem on a couch with the TV facing directly at him, and after a while he got up and swiveled the huge *Sony Trinitron* directly towards us. We all sat there and watched *Roots* until the next commercial break, which, by the way, Willem de Kooning muted with his remote, along with all the other commercials, I might add. During the break, his daughter Lisa turned to him and said, "But Bill, how can you see the TV from that angle?" He pondered this before replying, "I can use my imagination." Indeed.

So, I've met three great painters in my life, one was shy, pale and answered every question "Great" (Andy Warhol), one was considerate, thoughtful and surprisingly witty (De Kooning) and one was a brat (Basquiat). And they were all hugely talented, undeniably ahead of their time, and their work will surely live on, their names immortalized. And their paintings, of which sadly I have none, sell for gazillions of dollars today. Somewhat grudgingly, I have to admit that Jean-Michel Basquiat did succeed in capturing the zeitgeist of the deteriorating, crime-ridden yet extremely cool New York City of the 1980's and, I suppose, I should have been complimented that he had heard of me at all, that I was famous enough for him to even bear me a resentment. But I've been a brat myself, and I know the *high* in being one, and I've said a lot of stupid, pretentious things I now regret. Once, while at an interview during the maelstrom of media attention surrounding *Aquashow*, a journalist asked me what I thought of the current state of affairs in popular music. Today, while people may be quick to call the 1970's the golden age of rock music, I am even quicker to remind them that although great albums were being made, the most popular song of 1973 was *Tie A Yellow Ribbon*

Round the old Oak Tree and, don't get me wrong, it's a catchy tune and I've got nothing against it. Highbrow or low, popular music lives in a very big tent indeed, and there is room for both *Tony Orlando and Dawn* and *Leonard Cohen*.

But back then, when I was twenty-four, I wasn't so wise, and I said something to this journalist that I immediately came to regret. At the time, 1950's teen idol Neil Sedaka was making a very successful comeback with his *Sedaka's Back* album and I said something stupid and disrespectful about it, like *why is he coming back?* thinking I was smart, cute, hip, etc. And then just days later I was at a party for *RCA Records* and Neil Sedaka, the man himself, was introduced to me and he was absolutely one of the warmest and friendliest artists I ever met. Let me tell you, I felt like *schmuck*, and Neil, if you're reading this I hope you accept my *mea culpa*.

When Robert Hilburn called me *The First Intellectual of Punk Rock,* I thought it was an oxymoron. But now I believe I was some kind of a punk, at least in my attitude, before that word grew into a musical genre all unto itself. The punks were famous for saying what's on their mind, no matter how foolish it might read half a century later. It's a short distance from punk to grunge, which finally produced a brilliant songwriter, a true musical talent in *Nirvana's* Kurt Cobain, but he just took the *nihilist* pose too far. In March of 1994, I was playing in Rome when Kurt overdosed and went into a coma while in that same city. I'd been clean and sober for almost ten years and I wanted to speak to him, tell him *something* that might save his life and even tried to contact him at the hospital through my Italian promoter. But I never even got close to spreading the message to Kurt and within a month he was dead, blew himself away with a rifle in his hillside Seattle home. But really, even if I had been given an audience with Kurt and granted a few minutes to stand in front of his hospital bed, what would I have said? Don't make the same mistakes as me, man! That rarely works ...

To sum it all up, I can say, not in a shy way[2], that *Aquashow was* better than nearly anyone else's first album at that time and deserved the praise it received. Of course, I don't take full credit for that as there were many others involved, Peter Siegel and the great musicians he assembled but its certainly better than any other singer-songwriter's first album that I can think of, and the critics were backing me up on that. It was more original then Bob Dylan's first album, which contained mostly covers, but if it was as monumental as *Blond on Blond* to which the critics were comparing it to at the time, his masterpiece, and, I might remind you, his *fifth album*, well, I'd have to say, obviously not. And how do you rate one record against another anyway? But if the powers that be were making me believe I was better than *Bob* at that moment in time, then I was ready to wear that *thorny crown*, maybe even try to save suburbia as that ad agency believed I might. As we all know, Bob Dylan pulled out of his *slump*, the guy's got more artistic lives then a cat, and went on to achieve so many high-water marks in his career that it's difficult to count; deservedly being awarded the *Nobel Prize for Literature*. But I was stuck with the tag, from a particular time, when rock journalists were searching for a new Dylan and it trails me like a horny dog to this day. In a way it's annoying because I don't believe that the thirty-five plus albums I've released since my first have gone in any recognizable *Dylanesque* direction or style and yet at the same time, I'm proud to wear it. And who can deny that when you compare the actual recorded music of any of the *new Dylan's* you will not find much of a common thread besides it all being original, memorable and *good*.

The truth is that being called the *new Bob Dylan* was not a curse at all because I can say that nearly anybody who ever had the honor of belonging to that club, and that not only includes Bruce but also such fine singer-songwriters as Louden Wainwright and John Prine, is still working today Far from being a curse, it was a guarantee of lifetime employment. What I think those journalists were really trying to say was that we were all modern songwriters who were writing different kinds of songs, particularly lyrically, then what usually arrived in their crowded mailbox of new releases, the same as Bob Dylan himself had always written *different* kind of songs. More damning then that, in my case was that I committed the cardinal *American sin*: I did not become hugely successful when I was *supposed* to, when all the signs pointed that way, when the God of celebrity tapped me on the shoulder and whispered in my ear - *Go for it!*

Somehow or other I seemed to have blown my chance at megastardom and I can't blame it on drugs or booze or anything really, I mean others have made more mistakes then me both personally and professional and still gone on to pick up *Grammy* awards and fill stadiums. No, for some reason, I didn't *click* with a massive public. I have individual fans who are as fanatical for my music as any Bruce Springsteen or Tom Petty fan ever was for theirs, but my message didn't spread and I don't believe America knows how to celebrate *cult* artists like me; in fact it mostly ignores them, until they're dead and gone and the day finally arrives when society can re-invent them, claim ownership, and put *Robert Johnson* or *Edgar Allan Poe* on a postage stamp for all the world to see American Grade A culture at its finest.

And yet, in spite of it all, when I'm going through one of my dark days and all my failures, my lost opportunities, my continual struggles are relentlessly mocking me, my son Gaspard, also a professional musician now, tells me to *cut it out, Dad!* And reminds me that I fit into that slim ten-percent of music makers – and that includes everyone from Madonna to Paul McCartney to DJ David Guetta– who actually make a living from their music, selling albums, giving concerts, staying in the *game*.

I would even argue that the *rock star* label has undeniably lost much of its cache, to the point that by now, it has entered the international lexicon as a job description for just about anyone who does their job well and is praised for it: politician, architect, chef or plastic surgeon – they can all be rock-stars today. That the term itself has de-evolved over the last half century can also be attributed to the reality that truly iconic rock performers such as Mick Jagger or Bruce Springsteen or Bono or Lady Gaga are so much more than mere mortal rock stars, they're nothing less than *Rock Gods, Rock Supernovas, Rock Constellations*. Call them whatever you want, but at that level of fame they've reached a point where just their name itself defines the music they do and not vice versa. I've stood on a stage with Bruce Springsteen and looked out over a vast multitude of eighty-thousand euphoric fans and I can tell you, it's pretty close to feeling like a master of the universe until you are reminded that you're standing next to someone who really is. Whatever didn't happen in my career, I can too easily blame on short-sighted management or me just being too independent-minded, unable to march to the corporate step of the music business, but it is what it is. Rock musicians may credibly play the role of *rebel without a cause* on stage and in the media but when it comes down to the nitty-gritty of working within the confines of the establishment that runs so much of the music business, especially radio back in the day, they tend to toe the line as obediently as any middle manager. And then there comes that age, when after dropping our bad habits behind us, somewhere down that *stoned* trail, we turn into solid citizens, acknowledged by cultural institutions; fine family men and women, who stop on a dime at every worthy cause that passes us by if our name is spelled right. And I'm no different. As David Bowie and John Lennon sang, *Fame! What you want is in the Limo!*

My problems with alcohol and drugs ended over thirty years ago and my first four albums have gone on to attain something akin to *classic* status in spite of their modest sales at the time of their release. Today, with thirty-five plus albums to my name and over twenty-five hundred live shows under my belt, I'm still in the game, which says something about my ability to survive in a business where, as I've stated, success can be measured by just that - survival. Perhaps that's my greatest talent after all, more than being a gifted and prolific songwriter or an enduring road warrior or a singer with a memorable voice. *A survivor*. This is how it works, when you are brand new and if you're any good , there's an immediate energy of excitement that will swoop you up and take you along on its magic carpet ride for a while, and you won't have to try too hard to justify your right to exist in the rock universe, when everyone is betting that you'll be *the next one* to set the world on fire. Then, decades later, when you're older, and hopefully in good enough shape to still be at it, still strumming that *damn* guitar and croaking out the lyrics to your multitude of songs, you've entered into what I call the *museum stage* and your accomplishments are renewed as people become keenly interested in all you've seen and done. After all, you're a witness to the *glory days,* a decorated veteran of the rock 'n roll wars, who made it back from the bloody trenches. But it's the middle years, when you're cast into the wilderness, neither new nor old, that are the toughest and I survived even those, although I do deserve a *Purple Heart* for living with tinnitus.

Twenty-five years ago, both of my ears started ringing at a shrill volume all the time, *twenty-four-seven*, and they haven't taken a day off since. They were ringing when I woke up this morning and they'll be ringing when I go to bed tonight. When I do my next show, I'll be wearing custom molded earplugs to block out 25dB of the sound and protect my fragile hearing, so my ears won't ring worse than they already do, so I don't have to take a *Xanax* to fall asleep, to keep my tinnitus from what us sufferers call *spiking*. Although I've lost quite a bit of hearing in the upper mid-range frequencies, right where electric guitars, cymbals and snare drums live, I'm still pretty good in the low and high frequencies and in controlled situations, such as a recording studio, I have no problem judging mixes. But when my Tinnitus is really bad, it often triggers the dreaded *hyperacusis*[3], and sound itself becomes my enemy. One loud snare drum can set my head reeling for hours and then even the most banal noise, a knife dropped on a plate, a plastic bottle being crumpled, a car horn honking, even a baby crying, can be intolerable. Imagine a painter who has become allergic to paint, a sculptor who can't stand the feel of clay, and a director who hates actors. But I truly love music and I depend on it to keep me standing straight with a smile as the psychic winds of the infinite cosmos swirl around me. I'm not alone by any means, as many musicians of my generation, before the importance of *protecting your hearing* became known, struggle with Tinnitus as I do, and now we share this damned affliction with returning veterans of modern warfare; where a roadside bomb can reach a sound level of 175dB, and also with hunters who cradled shotguns next to their ears for too long. There's even a bunch of ordinary drugs that can trigger tinnitus as well, and that includes *aspirin*. As for me, I'm praying for a medical miracle; I don't want to die with my ears ringing. Or probably more accurately, when they do stop ringing I'll know I'm finally dead.

SIDNEY STEWART[4], A WELL-KNOWN PSYCHOANALYST I USE TO see in Paris, once confirmed to me that I am *American* from head to toe and supposedly, he also treated Tennessee Williams, so I guess he ought to know. Sidney was a long-time Paris resident, an expatriate like me, originally from Oklahoma, who chose to live his life in Paris after being captured by the Japanese in the Philippines during the earliest days of World War II, surviving the *Bataan Death March* and spending the remainder of the war in various Japanese prisoner of war camps where eighty percent of his fellow prisoners died. Understandably, he didn't take any of my problems too seriously. I only saw him for a year or so, but Sidney was a very wise man and inspired me in many ways so that when I wrote my western novel *Poetic Justice* years later, I set it in Oklahoma and dedicated it to him. It was the story of a young boy, *Petit Jean,* who was living on the frontier in the 1870s when he saw his father murdered by a Confederate zealot. He goes to live at his uncle's swanky bordello, right off the docks of a bustling and brutal New York where he meets poet Walt Whitman, a favorite of his mother who is now alcoholic and married to the man who killed his own father. *Petit Jean* is transformed into *John Little,* a dandy paid contract killer, who loves poetry, meets Theodore Roosevelt, fights in the Spanish-American War, and is plagued with thoughts of revenging his father's murder. *Poetic Justice* was published in three languages, French, Spanish and Italian, and really was inspired by the classic Sergio Leone westerns of the 1970's. It's a novel with a soundtrack[5], just waiting to be made into a film.

Sydney Stewart passed away at seventy-eight from emphysema, the result of forced labor in a Japanese *coral* mine during the war and the last time I saw him he was breathing only with the help of a nearby oxygen tank. If I would have known he was going to leave us so soon, I would have seen him more often because he was one of the wisest men I ever met when it came to insights into human nature. In spite of the absolutely hellish time he experienced during the war, he bore no grudge against the Japanese, saying that for centuries it was just part of their culture to mistreat any warrior who was captured. Sydney was always upbeat with an almost maniacal grin and was of enormous help when it came to getting through the cultural shock of living among the French in their country. Sidney ended my last session with some good advice, *stick with the music,* which I've done.

In spite of my ingrained and inescapable *American-ness*, I've chosen to live in France for almost thirty-years, but I never really rejected America or its culture and the great advantages it gave me. Obviously, the European life-style agrees with me and there came a point in the late 1980's when I came to the realization that if I wanted to continue on working in my chosen field, this was the obvious and only move to make. I had fans spread out all over the continent and in Scandinavia, solid relations with Patrick Mathe, owner of *New Rose Records* in France and other independent record companies beyond who would release and promote my records, respected journalists who would review my work fairly and regularly, and perhaps most importantly, I was looking for a French girl, a lovely actress who had stayed on my mind in spite of not seeing her for over six years.

It was 1983 when my band and I had just finished playing a show in Caen, which is the nearest city to the D-Day beaches, when I first laid eyes on Françoise, the love of my life. Of course, in a small

French city like that, there was one restaurant that served food after midnight and that's where we headed, three hungry musicians. I remember the restaurant as being nearly empty except for a small crowd sitting at a round table right next to where we were seated. As I recall it (although Françoise's version differs) the *jolie fille* sitting among this group made numerous trips to the ladies room, walking right past our table in a short skirt and tight-fitting green sweater. The second or third time she passed, Ernie Brooks my bassist turned to me and said loud enough for her to hear, *Now that's nice!* Françoise stopped in her tracks and smiled, *What's nice?* she asked, although I suspect she knew we were talking about her.

Luckily Ernie is a good talker with girls or anyone else and soon the two tables were immersed in wine, laughter and our bad French. We managed to understand that they were a group of actors, touring with a show called *A Capello Acapulco*, and the pretty girl's name was Françoise. Not surprisingly, it was Ernie who got her number on the pretext that we would like to see the show sometime. As for me, I couldn't keep my eyes off of her and just kept staring, thinking, if I had a girl like that, well, everything might be okay. As Françoise recalls it, one of her fellow actors, Philippe Fretun, spotted us when we walked into the restaurant as he was a music lover. *That's Elliott Murphy*, he told the table, *he's a rock singer from America*. Also, according to her, our style was totally out of sync with the times, when everyone was into the 1950's look *Grease*; whereas all of us walked in with long hair and even longer *duster* cowboy style coats; she says when we entered it was like a scene from a Sergio Leone western film and she half-expected to see some tumbleweed blown in by the wind following along. Francoise and her group left before us and I said to Ernie, *if you want to keep playing with me you're gonna give me that number she gave you*. And he did, not so much out of fear of losing his gig but more so, I think, because his wallet was already over-full of matchbook covers, napkins and scraps of papers, all with French girls' names and a scribbled number underneath.

The next day, we were heading for Grenoble, near the Italian border, for another show and I called Françoise when we got there. She seemed pleased that I called, but fairly *nonchalant* about the whole deal but did agree to meet me for a tea if and when I returned to Paris. I said that would be sooner than she thought and I immediately insisted that the band head back to Paris even though it was hundreds of kilometers out of our way. Françoise and I did meet and had more than a tea at the *Hotel des Deux-Iles* on the ile Saint Louis in back of Notre Dame. Another week passed and there came another day off, and I again returned to Paris and we went to see a film together, Alain Resnais' *Providence*; the word itself being defined as *timely preparation for future eventualities*. Little did I know...

In the six years that followed, I had no communication from or with Françoise, so much happened and, in a way, *everything* that happened was indeed preparing me for my future eventualities. I went to Milwaukee, met Rita, cleaned up my act, got a steady job at *Pryor, Cashman, Sherman and* Flynn as a legal secretary and Rita and I, after suffering through the pangs of a long-distance relationship, finally got married and she moved to New York and began a career as a personal trainer and life-coach which, I believe, she has continued to this day. Rita was wonderful for me, she pressed the *re-start* button of my life, but we weren't meant to be married to each other and that became sadly obvious soon after she moved in with me in Manhattan. I said goodbye to my dark Gramercy Paris studio and all it represented, and we moved into a one-bedroom apartment on the 26th floor of a brand-new high-rise on Park Avenue South with morning light streaming in the windows. You could say I was awake.

Two years later, Rita and I separated, and I was thinking to myself, *is this what I got clean and sober for? Another divorce?* And then someone asked me the most difficult question in life when your demons, their fangs no longer buried deep in your psyche, have finally retreated. Actually, it was my friend and fellow singer-songwriter, Garland Jeffreys, who popped that question, I said I wanted to move to Paris. And very quickly the planet lined up, my karma got super-sized and I was on my way. It seemed that Garland had a friend who sublet her loft there, that just happened to be unoccupied and two weeks later I was turning the key and opening the door of a loft on *rue de Faubourg Saint Antoine*. I woke up the next morning to the sound of soaring French *Mirage* military jets flying overhead, leaving a trail of blue, red and white vapor. It was *Bastille Day*, France's equivalent to the fourth of July. What a welcome!

THAT FIRST YEAR IN PARIS, 1990 I PUT OUT MY FIRST LIVE album *Live Hot Point* featuring the great Chris Spedding on guitar, recorded at the *Hot-Point* festival in Switzerland and it was my best-selling album in France since *Just A Story from America*. I knew I had to do something special after that to announce my arrival. By a *simple twist of fate*, Ernie Brooks was also in Paris, living in the 16th Arrondisement with Delphine, his future wife. He would be my partner for my next album project, my *12th*. My plan was to write the songs for that album at almost the same time as we were recording *and* there would be no overdubs, everything done live. A new digital technology for recording had developed, the *DAT*, a two-track digital cassette, and *Panasonic* had created a portable *DAT* recorder that could be used all over the world which I had shipped from the USA while buying a *Tascam* mixing console and some other gear in Paris. "*12*" would be my first attempt at home recording. Some say *luck* is just a combination of experience and opportunity, and as luck would have it, Ernie met Roger Robindore and brought him into our sphere, another US expat, and a literal tech wiz who would engineer the whole album as well as supplying vintage *Neumann* microphones. Between Roger's gear and my own we managed to set up a recording studio in an adjacent loft on rue de Faubourg St. Antoine in the aptly named *Cour des trois freres*[6] The first song we recorded was *The Loser*, which was me, talking to myself in a slow waltz time, trying to figure out how my life's journey had led me to this place at this time:

Just A Story from America

I was looking for the answer like some fairy tale - Somebody said there's a man here - And all his life he has just failed - You only learn from the losers - Of this I am sure...

I started writing songs ferociously, like my life depended on it. Françoise was pregnant, and I was making my twelfth album. I thought 12 a lucky number – 12 step programs, 12 inches to a foot, 12 disciples – lots of reason. Roger converted the bathroom of a Bastille loft into a control room while Ernie and I sang and played. I brought in a small string section and an accordion player, I tried to get a Peruvian pipe ensemble to come up out the Metro to join us but on the appointed day they never showed up. Then we moved to Lausanne, Switzerland and my friend Marc Ridet allowed us to use his club *Dolce Vita*, as a daytime studio and we recorded even more songs. It would turn out to be a double LP and a single CD that I thought it would be my last release on vinyl. I was wrong because in 2018 I re-released three of my albums from the 1980's in beautifully remastered vinyl editions. And they stand up.

Just before embarking to France, I had received a *telex*[7], an invitation for me to participate in the *first-ever International rock 'n roll convention*, taking place in the ancient city of Taormina, on the island of Sicily. I had no idea what I was getting into, but the promoter sent a plane ticket and his offer was intriguing enough for me to go for it. When I arrived at *Catania Airport*, he was waiting for me at the airport with a large sign, THE FIRST INTERNATIONAL ROCK 'N ROLL CONVENTION WELCOMES ELLIOTT MURPHY! I was impressed. We shook hands and I began asking him about the festival, who else would be participating, hadn't he mentioned *Sting*? He looked at me peculiarly, *Only you Elliott!* The kick-off event of the *Rock 'n Roll Convention* was held in a sumptuous disco where everything except the dance floor was covered in red velvet. It was announced as a Q&A where, from a *privileged insider's* view, I would provide candid insights into the mysterious world of rock. I came out onto the stage and there before me was a large crowd of Sicilian girls, milling around the tables, dressed in miniskirts, waiting to greet me. I tell you, one was more beautiful than the next, a flock of young Sophia Lorens, and I, thinking this was the best day of my life, awaited the first question.

The microphone was handed to a raven-haired beauty with almond eyes and gravity-defying figure. She eyed me provocatively, "*Signor Murphy, tell me...do you know Madonna?*"

I ruefully shook my head, "*No, sorry, not really... Years ago, before she became big I use to see her hanging around a rehearsal studio in New York, but that's about as close as I ever got to Madonna.*"

I could tell by the look on her face that this sultry teenage beauty was truly disappointed. She said nothing and disappeared back into the crowd which quickly dispersed. There were no more questions, I had blown my credentials big time and soon the disco was empty. But at least I got a song out of it, *Sicily*, which was one of the first songs recorded for 12 and received a fair amount of airplay on the French national radio. The most important song on the album, and one of my few that began as pure poetry, was *On Elvis Presley's Birthday*; it came from a memory I had been carrying with me for twenty years or more of a day I had spent alone with my father, in another life, riding in his Cadillac...

I can't say that I love this place where I live
This particular geographic location
But I've grown use to it and now I miss it when I'm away
Of course, when I was a child my father would take me with him.
Down to the bowery where the bums were,
And in the restaurant supply stores.
He would buy shiny steel refrigerators and deadly looking stoves.
While I begged him to take me to the army navy surplus stores on
Canal Street
To buy some big dead bullets.

He wore a short corduroy jacket, an informal hat with a puff of feather

Just A Story from America

And he talked with his hands in his pants pockets jangling change

Driving in his Cadillac it was Elvis Presley's birthday
They said it on the radio and my father liked Elvis
And it was wonderful - it was wonderful
We drove through the black neighborhoods on Long Island's north shore when Elvis was alive

My father was from Brooklyn and the depression left its mark,
From picking up coal on the railroad tracks.
He didn't have a good word to say about Franklin Delano Roosevelt.

Later, I liked elegant hotel bars,
Where I could drink under F. Scott Fitzgerald skies.
The coolest of the cool.
Never a child on Elvis Presley's birthday,
My dead father jangling change.

This is an unreal city.
You can be anybody you want to be
When you're alone...

On Elvis Presley's Birthday was my bittersweet *adieu* to my father...

I SUSPECT THAT THE PARISIANS NOW THINK OF ME AS SPECIES *American*, sub-species, *New Yorker*; they've given up expecting me to speak perfect French (although I insist my French is passable) or know all of Moliere's plays (although, thanks to Françoise, who has played in many, I know a few) but they do give me credit for sharing their love of *culture*, an indescribable concept they hold sacred, much more so, I think, than Americans who are more fascinated with anyone's ability to make money, be it Pablo Escobar or Steve Jobs. The French also respect me for having been friends with Lou Reed for a while, and for being the *local* guy Bruce Springsteen invites on stage (sometimes even with my son Gaspard) when he plays in Paris. It's gotten to the point that I am regularly referred to as *the most French of American singer-songwriters* and I take that as a cherished compliment. The French do value culture but most of all, they love to be *right* before anybody else, to be the avatars who swoop down and discover important artists way before the rest of the world gets hip. It's one of their specialties along with wine and *foie gras*; I mean, give them credit - Edgar Allan Poe, John Cassavetes and Elliott Murphy. Wow!

Admittedly, I am a privileged immigrant, not coming from a third world country and with a solid career and connections to exploit once I arrived; always trying to follow Theodore Roosevelt's maxim: *Do what you can, with what you have, where you are.* The adjustment to settling down in France, albeit a country that is similar to America in many ways (world-class consumers, lovers of high tech, and a democratic system of government that was born out of a bloody revolution) had its *trials* and sometimes, I must confess, I have felt the *immigrant's rage* when I did not fully understand what was going on around me and regrettably took it out on those I was most dependent upon. In my case, that has usually been my patient wife Françoise, who has literally guided me through the French system, culture and lifestyle in every way imaginable. Sometimes my frustrations got the best of me, and I'd take it out on her, smashing a plate, even throwing a chair, and feeling terrible afterwards. Let me tell you, the key to a long-term marriage is *don't get divorced* and Françoise and I have stuck together through thick and thin, even managing to put our son Gaspard through college at *SUNY Purchase*, without him having to take a student loan and where he got his BA degree in ... music production. The apples don't fall far from the tree and he has produced many of my most recent albums better than I ever could have. The day we dropped him off at *Purchase* after loading him up with piles of sheets, pillows, blankets and towels at a nearby *Bed, Bath and Beyond,* (most of which I haven't seen since) was emotionally rewarding beyond belief and gave me a sense of *mission accomplished* while he, quite normally, wanting nothing more from us then to *move off* campus as soon as possible. Four and a half years later (he took a semester off to go on the road with both Bruce Springsteen and *Incubus* and work in their respective sound crews) we watched him graduate in cap and gown as New York Senator Chuck Schumer gave a rousing speech of encouragement to the assembled graduates and their guests. Witnessing Gaspard being handed his diploma I suspect was more rewarding than winning a Grammy myself. When people ask me if I own a summer cottage somewhere, a second home by the sea perhaps, I show them my son's college diploma. Like a lot of parents, I suppose, I consider that to be the greatest achievement of my life.

Now Gaspard and I are both SUNY[8] graduates as I myself received a degree in literature in 1985 from SUNY Empire State, after a 15-year hiatus, I might add. Barely getting out of high school in 1967, my only option had been to take summer courses at Nassau Community College and hopefully do well enough to be accepted full time in the fall semester. It was there that I learned nearly everything I know today about harmony and musical notation. For example, I know that in classical music *parallel movement* is a no-no while in rock 'n roll it's done all the time, almost guaranteeing a hit; think *Louie Louie.* Today, I can read and write music at a snail's pace, but it doesn't do me much good in the world of music I inhabit where hardly any players *read*. More importantly, I can speak the language of music and count bars and recognize time and key signatures and major and minor scales. I even can tell you what the *coda*[9], or *outro* as we call it, to a song is.

So let's say that I've entered the *coda* of my own life and hopefully it's a very long *outro* indeed. My life hasn't followed the pre-destined course I assumed it would; I never took French in high school and flunked Spanish twice and in spite of that I've spent most of my adulthood living in a foreign country, playing for audiences whose first language is not English. Sometimes I wonder why I didn't go the other way, out to the West Coast *Promised Land* as so many New Yorkers my age did. When I was a kid, I it seemed that everything I loved, everything I wanted to be a part of, came from California, be it surfing or Hollywood movies or George Barris[10] custom hot rods. Pop culture seemed to thrive there, and LA was my *Mecca*, my *Nirvana*, my *Disneyworld*. I'm convinced that someday I'll move to Venice Beach and do a backwards Jim Morrison trajectory – he died in Paris and started out in Venice Beach while I'll do the opposite. Maybe I'll drop dead while surfing; a wrinkly hundred-year old in a loose-fitting wetsuit on a vintage *Gordon and Smith* long board.

In my 1967 Garden City High School yearbook they called me the *Pioneer Surfer of GC* and I still remember a surf festival on Gilgo Beach at which the legendary *Duke Kahanamoku,* who brought surfing to California from Hawaii, was the guest of honor. It was the *flattest* day of the summer, not a wave in sight, and when they asked the *Duke* what he thought of Long Island, he said obviously amused, *It's very nice but there's no surf.* I still remember some rare summer days when my parents would drive me to Gilgo in our yellow *Oldsmobile* station wagon, my surfboard hanging out the back, me anxious to don my wetsuit and hoping there would be some waves. I have a cherished memory of them, walking on the beach together, holding hands, talking about what I don't know, while I waited for a wave to take my higher...

I've visited Jim Morrison's grave in Pere La Chaise cemetery only once, but I've passed by the building in the *Marais* district where he *gave up the ghost,* while soaking in a bathtub; patting myself on the back for having outlasted Jim in Paris. He lasted three months and I'm here almost thirty years. If you're a rich rock star junkie, Paris is not a good place to be when you have too much free time on your hands because the French will indulge your habits if you ask. Both Johnny Thunders and Stiv Bators of the punk band *Dead Boys* were here when I first moved over , and we hung out a bit. Stiv was a lovely guy, very different from his onstage persona of a gum spitting punk; soft spoken, intelligent, thoughtful, who tragically got hit by a car twice in the same day - *love me two times* as Jim use to sing – and died because he refused to go to the hospital. As far as I know, I'm the last American rocker who calls Paris home. *Le dernier de les vedettes de rock*[11]*!*

Chapter Thirteen

TOUGHER THAN THE REST

| Elliott Murphy and Bruce Springsteen 1977

*I*n 1992 I received an urgent call from *Sony Records France* telling me that Bruce Springsteen was on his way to Paris for a show (which I knew) and wanted to get in touch with me (which I didn't know!) Bruce and I go way back, we kind of started out together, attacking the bright lights of New York from opposite directions, he from New Jersey, me from Long Island. And for a while there, we were both tagged the *New Bob Dylan*. We first met at *Max's Kansas City* in 1973, introduced by Paul Nelson. I liked him then and I like him now. Since that time, I'd visited him at his house in New Jersey and he has even climbed five flights to spend some time with me at my Paris apartment, both of us standing on my terrace, looking out over the rooftops of Paris, talking about the old days. Just around the time that his album *Born in the USA* was selling double-digit *millions*, we took two of his racing bicycles and rode twenty-five miles from his residence in Rumson, New Jersey to Freehold, the blue-collar town where he grew up, and shared the stories of our lives. We found an unopened door at his former high school and snuck in after-hours until a janitor threw us out, not realizing he was giving the *bum's rush* to that school's most illustrious alumni ever. Bruce and I have even fished together, Tom Sawyer and Huck Finn style, in his well-stocked pond on his property where it was literally *impossible* not to catch a fish. On that bike ride, Bruce showed me a favorite secret place of his, just off the road to Freehold, a fenced preserve where retired circus animals lived out their non-performing days. I saw giraffes and elephants inexplicably grazing in the New Jersey suburbs; far, far from any Circus big tent. And I wondered, as we rode by and those giant animals gazed up at me, if there will one day be a similar place for retired rock stars; strumming *air guitars*, while imagining cheering phantom crowds of fans fading farther and farther into the distance.

Anyway, in 1992 Sony passed my number on to Bruce and he called me from London to ask if I would like to do perform one of my songs with him at *Bercy Arena* when he came to Paris. Talk about an offer you can't refuse! You can bet, Bruce being a man of his word, that's exactly what happened. Together, we performed perhaps my most well-known slow song, *Rock Ballad*, I sang the verses while Bruce joined me on the choruses and threw in some subtle guitar licks. His concert was sold out, of course, and packed with 18,000 wildly enthusiastic fans. Bringing me onto that stage before a crowd of that size was an exceedingly generous thing for Bruce to do and yet totally within his character; he's not only invited me but also many other of his *peer* musicians, who didn't rise anywhere near to his level of success, countless numbers of times. Maybe it's his way of sharing the wealth, but no other star of his caliber that I know of has ever made the same gesture and it means so much to those of us blessed with his friendship and solidarity. For a long time, Bruce had an assistant, his personal tour manager, always at his side, the late great Terry Magovern. A very big guy, former Navy Seal, with a stern presence that could be menacing to those who didn't know him, Terry had been with Bruce since the early days and it was his job to come get me in the dressing room and walk me to the stage when it came time to perform *Rock Ballad*. As we got closer to the stage, I could hear the crowd roaring and I was getting more and more nervous, probably visibly trembling, and doubting if I could really pull this off without making a fool of myself. Terry, sensing my jitters, stopped me in my tracks and placed his two large hands on my shoulders.

"*Just like the old days, Elliott,*" he said. "*Only a few more people.*"

The old days. It seems my life begins some new chapter every twenty years or so. The first ended when *Aquashow* was released and then that next phase was truly over when I moved to Paris and my son Gaspard was born and I guess I became an *adult* so to speak. Now at sixty-nine, I have a feeling I'm about to start something else although I'm not sure what it is, maybe film, maybe something entirely different. But I try to move slow and stay in the moment, because as I once sang in *Deco-Dance*, in what seem like another life with almost prophetic accuracy, *the past is the only thing that lasts if you move too fast.*

In 1996 after the release of *Selling The Gold*, which featured a duet with Bruce on *Everything I do, leads me back to you*, I was booked to play France's premier music TV show *Taratata* and once again, since I had used studio musicians on the album I quickly needed to put a band together and reached out to Jerome Soligny, a

Just A Story from America

French rock journalist and singer-songwriter whose debut album I had produced, to ask if he could recommend a guitarist who might *fit in* with my style and he suggested Olivier Durand, a Le Havre native like him. I knew Le Havre had a great tradition of rock 'n roll, I call it the *Liverpool* of France, and I gladly met with Olivier up at my apartment in Paris who said ... almost nothing! I didn't know then what I know now: that Olivier is a man of few words but enormous talents on the guitar. That meeting was soon forgotten, and I did the TV show with a mediocre band and even though *Love to America*[1] got the crowd up and dancing I knew I needed something better than that if I was to go out on tour. Then, out of nowhere, Olivier started to show up at gigs, almost inviting himself onstage, and we began to connect. Even though he was 17 years younger, we seemed to share the same roots: blues, Stones, Dylan; not so rare but he also loved almost everything about Tom Waits which was a good sign.

Now that inauspicious meeting with Olivier was over twenty years ago, and I've played more gigs with him than with any other musician I've ever worked with – I've *definitely* eaten more breakfasts with him then with my own wife. Our life on the road has become so second nature to both of us that we hardly need to rehearse. If I want to change the set, I tell Olivier to learn a couple of songs and then we polish them up during the sound check. We also have written many songs together, most notably *Ground Zero,* sung in both French and English, and a memorial to the victims of 9/11. Olivier is a phenomenal guitarist, capable of playing in almost any style but, and I think I can accurately say this, I am confident that I bring out the best in him when I produce his solos on my records; I know his remarkable strengths as a musician and always push him to play something *original* and melodic which fits the song, and not just another *Strat* player ripping off tired blues-based clichés. But most importantly, Olivier has the enormous talent to take direction and come out with something that is totally his own unique sound. We both play fine *Taylor* acoustic guitars through a variety of effects pedals and I don't think any other guitar duo sounds quite like us. We've even been accused of using *playback*, which of course we never do, as the combination of our guitars, voices and my harmonica playing can make the sound so dense, so rhythmic, so orchestral, that it's hard to believe all of that music is coming from two just musicians. It is ...

Some years ago, I started to put together an archive of all my shows. I'm well over two-thousand-five-hundred now and probably not quitting anytime soon. There were years when Olivier and I did over 100 shows a year and I have regrets about all the time I had to spend away from my wife and son but as my brother Matthew likes to remind me, *This is the life we chose!* Which is a quote from *Godfather II*, in case you didn't know...

Epilogue

Photo Credit: Claudia Revidat

My mother, Josephine, when she was in her late eighties, managed to *escape* from a rehab/nursing home in Westhampton, Long Island, following a congestive heart incident when her heartbeat went up to one-seventy, something my own heart often did when I was using cocaine back in the 1970's. She was spending the weekend at the home of my sister Michelle and her husband Robert, in Amagansett, when she suddenly felt nauseous and confused. An ambulance was called, which took her to nearby Southampton Hospital, where Lou Reed had died just a few years before, and then, after stabilizing, she was moved to *Westhampton Care Center*, a nursing home. My mother remembers little of this activity or any other recent events but tells me she often finds herself dreaming of her own mother: she is a child back in her bedroom in that boxy grey house next to that canal in Baldwin, Long Island, where I once fished for *snappers* and imagined myself to be *Huck Finn,* and she's asking her mother to come up and comfort her, something which, according to my mother, *her* mother never did. To make matters more confusing, my mother now insists she never loved either of her parents, which pains us, her three children, to hear as we remember both of them, as loving grandparents; gray-haired and from another era, who never had *Coca-Cola* in the refrigerator and always served ice water at meals. I can still remember the smell of my grandfather's WWI uniform *mothballed* in their attic and I know he spent time in France during that war and now I'm here, coming full circle in a way. And when I ask my mother, if she really didn't love her parents, why then did we often drive all the way down to the south shore to visit them in their little house on holidays, when, personally speaking, I would have much rather stayed in our sumptuous house in Garden City, alone in my room with my guitars and books? Well, she rationalizes, she imagines she was just trying to be a good daughter but regrets it now. I tell her she must have loved them once, but something changed inside her since. She insists no, she never loved them, and they didn't love her much either and that's it as far as she's concerned. But still, I'm not sure what the truth is. Even with my own story, as hard as I've tried to recollect things accurately and with fairness, I'm aware that my own emotional truth might have little basis in fact and that with hindsight the feelings surrounding those truths, stored securely in my memory, can change as drastically and imperceptibly as the colors of a sunset.

After living in France for nearly 30 years, I can't say the nursing homes are superior here – my wife Françoise's mother died in one recently – but at least the national health care system seems to run at the same speed for everyone regardless of income or resources and you kind of know what's going to happen to you when you're sick or disabled with the relief that there will be no battle with the bureaucracy, or need to empty your bank account, to get there. Just for the record, I can say that the - Securité Sociale as they rightly call it - at least during my years of living here, is efficient and as personal as any medical care I ever received in New York. Of course, a French doctor may not be the best specialist to consult about the dangers of smoking as I've seen plenty of them, standing outside hospital entrances still dressed in their operating scrubs, stethoscopes draped around the neck, puffing away.

The French have been very good to me, awarding me both the Medaille de Paris in 2012 and Chevalier de l'ordre des arts et des lettres in 2015. I have great respect for them as a people, their style and intelligence, and perhaps I have begun to understand them after nearly three decades of living among them. By their very nature, they are a highly analytical tribe, who like to draw conclusions of the significance, or lack of, in whatever they are examining, and then debate it over a glass of wine and fine meal. Even though I no longer drink wine, in an odd yet undeniable fashion, I seem to fit in here and I share their analytical DNA; that's really the thread that has run through everything I ever tried to create, trying to understand how I fit in. Someone said a life not examined is a life not worth living and perhaps I've taken that to extremes, but as someone else said, the definition of an expatriate is someone who feels more at home when he is not at home…and perhaps that's the best explanation as to who I am and why I'm here.

Before she retired from *Tiffany & Co.*, after working as a salesperson for twenty years, my mother would often return to her apartment on York Avenue and East 80th Street after work, crying that none of those people she was waiting on in the fine china department could ever imagine she had once dined at the White House with President Eisenhower, chatted with Bernard Baruch, met Liz Taylor and her producer husband Mike Todd and sat on singer Perry Como's lap. She had once been the wife of a famous man, my father, and now no one cared. But Mom, I would plead, you have to enjoy the life we have today. *You try working at Tiffany!* she said. I never did, of course, but I did write and record a song called *Diamonds by the Yard*, inspired by a piece of Tiffany jewelry and the glimmering night lights of Manhattan that I have sung it thousands of times, all around the world.

Many years ago, on that day when Bruce Springsteen and I rode bikes to his hometown, he asked me what I would want if I could have anything in this world. It was at the time of his *Born in the USA* rise to mega stardom, when it seemed every marvelous thing this world had to offer was coming to him at his demand. My immediate response, almost without thinking, was "Well … a hit record for one thing," probably saying that more out of jealousy than anything else. But Bruce was wiser than me and dismissively shook his head. "A hit record is something great, that's for sure, but it's not everything." I often wish he'd ask me that question again, because now I know what I'd ask for: "To see my father's face again, to talk with him."

My father is buried in *Evergreen Cemetery* in Brooklyn along with dancer Bill "Bojangles" Robinson, jazz saxophonist Lester Young, victims of the Triangle Shirtwaist Fire (which led to the unionization of garment industry employees) and countless others. In 1985, when I got sober, I went there on a pilgrimage to make amends, to say goodbye, to tell him my story, and was surprised and disappointed to still not find a gravestone.

"*I told you, we didn't believe in that sort of thing,*" explained my mother when I asked her. The name Elliott Murphy might be on thirty-five albums, but Elliott Murphy Sr. has no marking over his grave, so what is not there is what I'm ending with now:

ELLIOTT MURPHY, SR.
SEPTEMBER 5, 1917 - OCTOBER 19, 1965
The Aquashow - The Sky Club
Father to Matthew, Michelle & Elliott
Husband to Josephine

∽

Afterword

TIME FLIES

Memoirs, like the real lives they intend to mirror, are lopsided and far from symmetrical; often they can appear incomplete no matter how long they go on. But from the poet's point of view, a life unexamined may not be worth living so that was my original intention. That by writing these thousands of words, painfully recalling lost souls, bittersweet anecdotes and lessons learned too late in life, in addition to trying to express all the joy music has given me, it might help to give my own life, my story, a sense of value and purpose. And I can say it has done its job well. You see, I'm no different from you in my desire to be acknowledged for a life well done. For me, this (for now) finished process of stopping time and putting my fragmented memories down on paper has proven cathartic. A clear timeline has emerged marking the major and minor events of my personal and professional life, my joys, sorrows and struggles. What seemed like chaos before, now seems orderly; what seemed random, now seems neatly planned. But whether this memoir, or any other, actually resembles a real life, is hard to call. A book is one dimensional by nature and human existence is anything but that. Still, it is a daunting task to make sense of that part of my voyage already completed while

Afterword

that same voyage continues to move forward. Writing a memoir is like taking a seat on a mystery train where the past whizzes by on your left and the future unfolds on your right and you sit transfixed, always uncertain of your final destination. And then, a new reality suddenly emerges that colors all that came before it...

My mother Josephine passed away on December 7, 2018 in her apartment on York Avenue in Manhattan where she had lived these past forty-six years. She was 92 years old. A Long Island girl who always wanted to live in the city, she had achieved her dream. In fact, you could say that her permanent move into the bright lights – big city in 1972 paralleled my own career lift-off and you could also say it was because of her first steps into Manhattan that I was able to begin my treacherous climb up the rock 'n roll mountain. You see, when my mother left our last family house on Long Island, to move into the city, she had allowed my brother Matthew and I to stay behind and pay her a nominal rent. We quickly put together a band to rehearse in the basement and began our forays into the city in search of fame, fortune and most importantly, a record deal. If my mother hadn't provided us with that basecamp, I could never have started that aforementioned climb.

My mother liked to be called Jo, after the character in the Louise May Alcott novel *Little Women* (that I confess to never have read), because like her, she was a practical woman, responsible and capable, who had fought with her wildly fluctuating emotions to finally achieve, in her later life, a positive and loving relationship with this sweet old world. Undeniably, she had some tough breaks – an alcoholic father, losing her husband at 39, financial difficulties, disastrous loss of status and almost having to begin her life again when it was nearly half-way done. But she never gave up. In my view, she was always a fighter and a courageous one at that, although I don't know if she would have considered herself as such. Sometimes she triumphed in her battles, sometimes not, but through it all she was devoted to her children and even when all three of us were all well into adulthood,

Afterword

we retreated to spend time under her roof when our own lives temporarily collapsed. Her door was always open to her children.

As a young woman my mother was beautiful, with a vivacious personality and flaming red hair. She had wanted to be an actress and so naturally she found a life full of drama. Her own story, linked to a certain time and place in America, deserves a fitting biography and maybe I'll set my hand to that formidable task some distant day. Losing a parent at my age may be in the natural course of events but still there is an undeniable void hanging nearby, a shadow has appeared out of nowhere, that has now become part of my reality. I suppose, like everything else, I'll get use to it.

Time flies
We just walk
Long distance
Hello Mom
I just wanted to talk

That's from a song I wrote years ago. I'll say it again, my songs know more about me than I do about them. And mom, thanks for taking me to those guitar lessons; they really paid off. I love you.

| Josephine and Elliott Murphy

Notes

Prologue

1. **French** for the claimed reason for the existence of something or someone. I live in France, so these useful French phrases slip into my vocabulary almost involuntarily, much the same as today when a French person might prefer to say *weekend* rather than *fin de la semaine*. N'est pas?

Chapter 1

1. Named after **Nelson Rockefeller**, long term governor or New York State and short- term US Vice President after Nixon's resignation.
2. **Father Knows Best** was an American television comedy series, which portrayed a middle class family life in the Midwest and ran on television from 1954 to 1960. Never a favorite of feminists.
3. **Jimmy** was my boyhood nickname.
4. **The Ed Sulllivan Show** was the same TV variety show that introduced both Elvis Presley and The Beatles to America.
5. My father put the blame for this oversight on New York Parks Commissioner **Robert Moses,** which literally put his show out of business and around our house, Moses was the nemesis of the Murphy clan.
6. **Roosevelt Field** was originally an airfield and used by aviation pioneer Charles Lindbergh when he took off on his solo flight to Paris in 1927.
7. In later years, Charles Lindbergh's reputation has been much tarnished by his isolationist stance prior to World War II and purported anti-Semitism as recounted in Philipp Roth's 2004 novel ***The Plot Against America***.
8. To know what a **Hammond B3** sounds like at its best, just listen to Steve Winwood's mind-blowing organ intro to *Gimme Some Loving*.
9. **Que reste-t-il de nos amours**? was a French popular song, with music by Léo Chauliac & Charles Trenet and lyrics by Charles Trenet that was used extensively in the François Truffaut film Stolen Kisses (1968). The song is best known to English-speaking audiences as "I Wish You Love", with new lyrics by Albert A. Beach. Ironic that my parent's favorite song would actually have a French origin.
10. Named after **Alexander Turney Stewart** (1803 – 1876), a successful Irish entrepreneur who made his multi-million dollar fortune in what was at the time the most extensive and lucrative dry goods business in the world as well as founding Garden City. Far from the Donald Trump of his day...
11. The **Rorschach test** is a psychological test in which subjects' perceptions of inkblots are recorded and then analyzed using psychological interpretation,

complex algorithms, or both. I would have done better if I'd been *stoned*, I'm sure, but I was only 10 years old.

12. ***I Am Curious (Yellow)*** is a 1967 Swedish film written and directed by Vilgot Sjöman, that was actually banned in prim and proper Massachusetts at the time of its release. Aside from some fairly mild sex scenes, the film featured interviews with Martin Luther King and footage of Russian poet Yevgeny Yevtushenko who I actually hung out with in Italy and Paris many years later.

13. A **soapbox racer** is a motor-less vehicle which is raced on a downhill road either against the clock or against another competitor propelled by the first, and still free, energy source – gravity!

14. **The Dead-End Kids** made six films for Warner Bros, including *Angels with Dirty Faces*, with some of the top actors in Hollywood, including James Cagney (to whom I sent a letter and received an autographed photo I still have) and Humphrey Bogart.

15. **Clapton is God** was a common graffiti sprayed across London walls in the late 1960's

16. When the drinking age was still 18, **College Mixers** were held to introduce the students of the local schools to each other, music, dancing and booze.

17. In true synchronicity, I am writing this from room 130 in the *Stadshotellet* in Karlstad, Sweden, the **"Beatlesrummet"**, which is actually where John and Paul slept one night on their Swedish tour in 1963 just before going to the US and changing my life.

18. If you have any doubt of this be sure to catch **The Fog of War: Eleven Lessons from the Life of Robert S. McNamara**, a 2003 documentary film about the life and times of former U.S. Secretary of Defense Robert S. McNamara directed by Errol Morris.

19. The **Kent State shootings** were the shootings on May 4, 1970 of unarmed college students by members of the Ohio National Guard during a mass protest against the Vietnam War at Kent State University in Kent, Ohio. Twenty-eight guardsmen fired approximately 67 rounds over a period of 13 seconds, killing four students and wounding nine others. But it took a Canadian, Neil Young, to write the haunting song *Ohio* about these tragic American events.

20. In 1988 I received a Bachelor of Art degree in literature from **Empire State College**.

21. **Mike Bloomfield** was the lead guitarist of *The Paul Butterfield Blues Band* and died of a heron overdoes in 1987 at the age of 37.

22. By the **13th Floor Elevators**, of course.

23. Fellow Long Island musician **Billy Joel** also played at the 305 *Lounge* with his band *The Hassles*.

24. **Post-Traumatic Stress Disorder**

25. In Long Island waters **snappers** are baby bluefish. I was once taking my son fishing for them in East Hampton and some guy walked by and interrupted our good times by insisting that these were not **snappers**. If you're reading this, you're a jerk!

26. The **Methodists** held huge yearly conventions in Ocean Grove, New Jersey which is next to Asbury Park, Bruce Springsteen's hometown, but they did not convert any members of the Springsteen clan as far as I know.

Notes

27. **Jayne Mansfield** (1933 – 1967) was a major Hollywood sex symbol during the 1950s who was known for her wardrobe malfunctions long before Janet Jackson popped out her nipple at the 2004 Super Bowl half-time show in Houston, Texas. Jayne would have been proud.
28. **Arthur Godfrey** (1903 –1983) was an American radio and television broadcaster who had absolutely nothing to do with Jayne Mansfield as far as I know.
29. In *The Great Gatsby*, narrator Nick Carraway tells Jay Gatsby, "You can't repeat the past," to which Gatsby assuredly replies, "Why of course you can."
30. In Orson Welles classic film *Citizen Kane*, they key to understanding Kane's relentless ambition seemed to be the loss of his treasured childhood sleigh *Rosebud*.

Chapter 2

1. And if you are in any doubt about the Universe's sense of humor, at about the same time I was playing in Bang Zoom, Bruce Springsteen was playing in **Doctor Zoom and the Sonic Boom**.
2. About *you know who* and long before Elton John's **Candle in the wind**.

Chapter 3

1. The term **drinking the Kool-Aid** refers to the 1978 tragic death of over 900 of Jim Jones cult followers in Guyana who committed mass suicide together in a belief they were going to a better world.
2. I briefly met the late Rolling Stones' muse **Anita Pallenberg** in Paris when I hooked up with Anna Sui, world class fashion designer and once friends back in the day when we would go to the **Mudd Club** together. But I didn't have the nerve to say much to Anita.
3. Bruce Springsteen's preferred destination for those who were **Born to Run**.
4. **Haight-Ashbury** is a district of San Francisco, known for being the birth of, hippie counterculture.
5. **A&R** (Artist and Repertoire) – the gatekeepers of the major record labels when it comes to signing artists.
6. Just to be clear, there is *New York City* which is composed of 5 boroughs – Manhattan, Queens, Brooklyn, Bronx & Staten Island - and is located in *New York State*. But when I talk about **New York**, in rock 'n roll geography, I'm talking about *New York City* and more specifically *Manhattan* and probably even more specifically, that part of Manhattan below 14th Street.

Chapter 4

1. **Everything is an Afterthought**: The Life and Writings of Paul Nelson by Kevin Avery.

Notes

2. **Lord & Taylor** is a New York based department store, with branches all over the country.
3. I later found out that the **Birdcage Café** was among Andy Warhol's favorite lunchtime spots, so finally it wasn't so uncool after all.
4. **Acetate Discs** were once the favored medium for comparing different takes or mixes of a recording, and before vinyl copies of a new release were available, acetates were often used as preview copies for important journalists and radio Disc Jockeys.
5. **Lou Reed** called my mother because by this time she was living in the city and it must have been the only contact number Paul had for me.
6. Years later I auditioned for Milos Forman for the lead in the film version of **Hair**. He cut me off in the midst of my singing and gave the part to John Savage. But I forgave him.
7. **Glam rock** (also known as **glitter rock**) is a style of rock music that developed in the early 1970s, and was performed by singers and musicians who wore outrageous clothes, makeup, and hairstyles, particularly platform-soled boots and glitter. Glam rock peaked during the mid-1970s with artists including David Bowie, Roxy Music, Alice Cooper, New York Dolls, Lou Reed and Iggy Pop. The more I think about it, I was really not glam rock in any way shape or form.
8. At the conclusion of **Raiders of the Lost Ark**, Indiana Jones is assured that the *Ark of the Covenant* is in a "safe place" and the scene cuts to shots of the Ark being wheeled away into the depths of a very large and ominous looking warehouse full of similarly marked crates ... probably full of demo tapes.
9. **The Partridge Family** was an enormously successful TV series about a widowed Mom and her kids who embark on a music career, which ran from 1970 – 1974 and produced David Cassidy, that era's version of Justin Bieber.
10. **Shindig!** was an American rock 'n roll variety TV series which aired on ABC from 1964 to 1966 and apart from appearances by almost every major group or singing star of the day from The Beatles on down also featured a sexy dance troupe called the Shin-diggers, to inspire the bands.
11. **Duke's Coffee Shop** was located in the Tropicana Motel, long term residents included Tom Waits and Iggy Pop. It has since relocated.

Chapter 6

1. From **All The Young Dudes**, written and produced by David Bowie and recorded with perfection by *Mott the Hoople*.
2. David Bowie actually used this phrase in the lyrics of his song **Station to Station**.
3. The only non-Stones artist **Rolling Stones Records** ultimately signed was Reggae legend *Peter Tosh*.
4. In Manhattan real estate lingo, **pre-war** denotes classy buildings with high rents built before WWII. In Paris, on the other hand, it could mean before the *French Revolution*.
5. **American Association of Retired Persons** – I'm still not a member and neither, I believe, is Mick Jagger.

Notes

Chapter 7

1. **Sweet Jane**, performed by the Velvet Underground on their 1970 album *Loaded*, was written by band's leader, Lou Reed, and has been covered by Mott the Hoople and perhaps most memorably by the Canadian band Cowboy Junkies whose own lead singer, Margo Timmins, turned it into sultry ballad.
2. Ironically, Lou Reed went on to sign with **Arista Records** himself where he released *Rock and Roll Heart*. The rumor is that this deal saved Lou from bankruptcy.
3. Upon meeting **Huntington Hartford** (1911-2008) at JG Melons, Geraldine and I were invited to his Sutton Place townhouse to play *double-up*, which we knew nothing about and suspected was some sort of change sex partners game as Hunt was always surrounded by beautiful, sensual, and to my eyes at least, *willing* girls. Turned out it was just a double-sized ping-pong table with big rackets and balls!
4. The **Motion Picture Production Code** (popularly known as the Hays Code) was the set of industry moral guidelines that was applied to most United States motion pictures released by major studios from 1930 to 1968. It obviously did not apply to the *other* Hollywood, that of the Porn Industry, thriving just over the hills in the San Fernando Valley.
5. **Dan Tana's** was a movie and rock star hang-out on Santa Monica Boulevard, where many a night I saw Harry Dean Stanton standing at the bar looking very content.
6. **The Ghost of Christmas Future**, is a fictional character in English novelist Charles Dickens's *A Christmas Carol*, closely resembling the Grim Reaper.

Chapter 8

1. According to Ernie Brooks, once the **Modern Lovers** album was finally finished, Jonathan called Warner Bros to announce that they would not be performing any of the songs contained on that album in concert.
2. Although I first recorded **Drive All Night** with my Boston band, it didn't make it onto an album until 1977's ***Just A Story from America***, done with British musicians. But when I listen back now, I like the first version better. Damn!
3. The **Skebopuben** in Skebobruk, a great little club where I have played many times, and holds the dubious distinction of cancelling a show by The Beatles in 1962 when the booker of the club found out they were not from London.
4. **Andy Paley**, whose father worked as a publicist for my father's *Aquashow*, eventually produced his favorite songwriter's comeback album *Brian Wilson* in 1988.
5. Now I drink *Ginger Ale* and *Diet Coke,* but mostly **Perrier** and in 1977, I put *Perrier* into the lyric of my song, *Summer House,* even before I even moved to France.
6. The best compliment I ever received about my songwriting was when Bruce Springsteen was interviewed for the documentary, ***The Second Act of Elliott***

Murphy and said, *"Elliott wrote songs that sounded like hits but weren't hits for some reason"*.
7. She eventually upgraded from the **Maverick**.
8. The **Five Towns** is an informal grouping of villages and hamlets in Nassau County, United States on the South Shore of western Long Island. The area is one of the wealthiest in New York State and has one of the highest percentages of Jewish residents in the nation.
9. **Isadora Duncan** (1878 - 1927) was an American dancer who was acclaimed throughout Europe. Born in California, she lived in Western Europe and the Soviet Union from the age of 22 until her death at age 49, when her scarf became entangled in the wheels of an **Amilcar CGSS** sports car in which she was riding. Supposedly, Zelda Fitzgerald threw herself down a flight of stairs when Scott flirted with Isadora in the south of France.
10. **Nick Carraway** is the disillusioned narrator in F. Scott Fitzgerald's *The Great Gatsby* (1925), a position gained solely due to him coincidentally living right next door to Jay Gatsby's over-the-top mansion in a very modest cottage in fictional West Egg; a nouveau riche village on Long Island's north shore supposedly modeled after Kings Point where my Uncle Arthur, a Gatsby-like character too, lived.

Chapter 9

1. **Swinging London** is a catch-all term applied to the fashion and cultural scene that flourished in London in the 1960s. It consisted largely of music, discotheques, fashion and celebrity drug busts.
2. Before Sony bought Columbia, Epic and other labels they were all under the umbrella of **CBS** who also owned radio and television stations.
3. Many years later, when I was clean and sober and sitting in the back seat of a yellow cab in NYC a familiar voice turned around to say hello to me. The driver was my ex-coke dealer, now with a new name and enrolled in the **Federal Witness Protection Program**.
4. Love that word! If you Google ***eponymous***, you'll see that it means when a person or character or even a rock band gives their own name to something. *Huckleberry Finn* is an eponymous novel; Bob Dylan's first album *Bob Dylan* also fits the bill. And it rhymes with hippopotamus which is not easy to do.
5. The city of **Paris** is divided into twenty Arrondisements and each one has its own *Mairie* or city hall. The one in the 6th arrondisement, located almost right next store to Catherine Deneuve's apartment overlooking Place Saint Sulpice, is particularly opulent. Take a visit next time you come over.
6. **David Bailey** wouldn't give his permission to use the real photo for any ads, only for the album cover itself.
7. What we called the monolithic CBS headquarters on 6th Ave; after the Spencer Tracy film ***Bad Day at Black Rock***.
8. Like Bruce Springsteen, my first guitar was a made in Japan **Kent**, candy apple red with three pickups and terrible action! I have never loved any instrument as much as I did this, *my first love*.

Notes

Chapter 10

1. I've also had the pleasure of getting to know the legendary co-star of **Cabaret,** the timeless Marissa Berenson, who like me lives in Paris, and who will appear in my film *Broken Poet*.
2. **West Egg**, (actually a pseudonym for *Great Neck*, Long Island) is the setting of *The Great Gatsby* while **Fear and Loathing in Las Vegas** was the title of Hunter S. Thompson's most famous work.
3. Blondie was the lead voice on Beach Boys hit ***Sail on Sailor***.

Chapter 11

1. **Robert Lowell** (1917 – 1977) was an American poet who could trace his origins back to the *Mayflower* and taught at Harvard.

Chapter 12

1. ***Roots*** (1978), the story of a black American's slave origins based on the book by Alex Haley was perhaps the first successful mega-series on TV long before *The Sopranos* or *Breaking Bad*.
2. From Frank Sinatra's ***My Way*** (English lyrics by Paul Anka)
3. **Hyperacusis** is a health condition characterized by an over-sensitivity to certain frequency and volume ranges of sound (a collapsed tolerance to usual environmental sound). A person with severe hyperacusis has difficulty tolerating everyday sounds, some of which may seem painfully loud to that person but not to others.
4. Sidney Stewart's book, "***Give us this Day***" recounts his story
5. In the Spanish version, **Justicia Poetica**, I included a CD with three *soundtrack* songs.
6. Courtyard of three brothers.
7. **Telex** were Pre-email, pre-fax, prehistoric ...
8. State University of New York
9. In music, a **coda** is a passage that brings a piece to an end. Think *Leading to your door* from *The Long and Winding Road*.
10. **George Barris** also designed the *Batmobile*. I bought a toy model of one for Gaspard when he was a kid.
11. A literal French translation of *Last of the Rock Stars*.

Chapter 13

1. Another unintentionally prophetic song of mine which mentions not only **Bill Cosby sit com blahs** but also country music turning ***swift*** ... as in Taylor!

About the Author

Elliott Murphy has released over thirty-five albums of original music since his debut album AQUASHOW (1973) and continues to perform concerts in Europe, Japan, Canada and the USA. His writing has appeared in Rolling Stone (U.S.), Vanity Fair (France) and other international publications.

Born in 1949 to a show business family in New York, Elliott began his career with a troubadour like odyssey in Europe in 1971, which included a bit part in Federico Fellini's film *Roma*. His 1996 album SELLING THE GOLD featured an extraordinary duet with Bruce Springsteen who often invites Elliott on stage to perform with him during his European tours.

In 2015 Elliott Murphy was awarded the *Chevalier de l'Ordre des Arts et des Lettres* by the French Minister of Culture.

www.elliottmurphy.com

 facebook.com/elliott.murphy.16

Also by Elliott Murphy

Novels:
Poetic Justice

Marty May

Tramps

Short Story Collections:
Café Notes

Where the Women are Naked and the Men are Rich

The Lion Sleeps Tonight

Paris Stories

Poetry:
Forty Poems in Forty Nights

The Middle Kingdom

Printed in Poland
by Amazon Fulfillment
Poland Sp. z o.o., Wrocław

25889773R00120